CHELL E.W.
ESSINGER L.
ONEY L.
ORE C.G.
ORE J.G.
RAN J.P.
RGAN W.G
RRIS A.M.
RRIS E.T.
RRIS R.D.
RROW G.H.
RT R.C.P.
TTLEE H.E.
UNTAIN C.B.
HOLLAND L.W.
NFORD F.A.
NNS P.
RPHY K.F.
RPHY S.E.
RRAY P.C.
ERS C.D.
H W.J.R.
LSON F.A.
VTON M.J.H.
HOLLS S.T.A.
HOLS M.A.M.
HOLSON E.C.
BBS A.B.K.
ONAN L.
ASS S F
EA J.
ONNELL R.L
ONOHUE E J
EEFE C.C.W
VE E.R.J.
MARA T.
ER W.J.
MER H.W.
WORTH L.J.
TERSON T.B.
NE A.
NELL A R
PER G.D.
KS A T
RY E J
LPS A.S.
LLIPS W.J.
LLIPS W.N.
TER A.B.

VALPIED J.H.
VAN-GELDER F.
VENESS K.W.D.
WADE N.T.

WORLAND N.C.
WRIGHT J.J.
YOUNG D.G.C.
ZIMMERMAN J.P.

2/21 BATTALION

ADAMS H.G.
ADAMS J.W.
ADAMS R.G.
AINGER A.F.
AINSBURY W.
ALFORD F.W.
ALI M.
ALLEN H.R.
ALLEN H.W.
ALLEN L.A.E.
ANDERSON I.T.
ANDREWS A.J.
ARCHIBALD H.P.
ARGUS E.S.J.
ARMSTRONG J.F.
ARNELL E.M.
ARROWSMITH W.C.
ASHWORTH D.W.
AUSTIN G.W.
BAILEY H.
BAKER T.L.
BALCOMBE R.M.
BALL A.P.
BALL N.T.
BALLINGER O.J.
BANKS C.R.
BANKS D.N.
BARBOUR R.E.
BARCLAY R.A.
BARNES R.G.
BARNES W.H.
BARR D.J.
BAYFIELD M.
BEATTIE A
BEATTIE R.E.
BEEL F.F.
BEGNONE J.A.
BEGNONE R.J.
BELL H.
BELL I.P.
BENDLE A.L.
BENNETT E.T.
BENNETT R.A.

CLELAND H.R.
CLERKE A.C.
COATES K.B.
COLEE R.W.
COLHOUN C.S.
COLLINS A.J.
COLLINS G.F.
COLLINS S.C.
COMBEN A.N.
CONNELLAN T.J.
CONNORS D.R.
COOK W.E.
COOKE L.W.
COOKE R.T.
CORNELL L.G.
COSTIN R.
COWELL E.A.
CRABB F.L.
CRABBE C.J.
CRAY G.W.
CRILLY J.
CROSHER A.
CROSS F.L.
CROSS R.F.J.
CURTIN R.
DAFF H.L.
DALTON L.
DARBY W.G.
DAVIDSON A.F.
DAVIS J.L.
DAVIS L.J.
DERBYSHIRE J.W.
DERMODY A.J.
DEVERE L.L.
DEW J.A.
DOBBYN S.G.
DOCKING E.W.
DOLL G.
DONALD D.J.
DOOLAN G.F.
DOOLAN W.T.
DOOLEY J.M.
DORGAN T.

HUTCHINS E.E.
HUTCHINS F.
HUTCHINS T.
HYNES R.S.
INKSTER S.F.G.
IRELAND J.H.
JACKSON D.K.
JACKSON M.
JACKSON N.
JACKSON S.A.
JACOBS P.A.
JACOBSEN C.P.
JAFFREY I.G.
JEFFERY S.T.
JOLLY A.F.
JONES F.R.
JONES G.L.
JONES H.S.
JONES P.
JORDAN F.H.
KAY B.G.
KEATING R.J.
KELLAM L.R.
KELLY B.M.
KELLY J.F.
KELLY R.G.
KELSO A.R.
KELTON C.J.
KENDALL E.A.
KENNEDY F.
KENNEDY F.E.
KENNEDY R.J.
KENT W.R.
KILMARTIN L.J.
KING A.W.
KINNAIRD J.T.
KIRKMAN W.J.
KNIGHT J.B.
KOFOED R.C.
LACEY C
LAFFERTY P.J.
LAMB L.
LAND A.F.C.
LANGER J.J.
LAPPIN A.G.
LAWRENCE H.
LAWSON K.F.
LAWTHER F.J.
LAZARUS S.A.
LEAHY W.J.

PASCOE A.K.
PATEN R.F.
PAYNTER C.N.
PAYNTER D.S.
PERRY D.G.
PINDER W.E.
PITMAN K.E.
PLUM H.L.
PLUMMER E.L.
PLUNKETT W.R.
POHLMAN G.F.
PORTER J.A.
PORTER J.M.
PORTHOUSE L.H.
POWELL H.F.
PRIDEAUX R.S.
PRINCE F.J.
QUARRELL E.J.
QUIGLEY G.G.
RAINSBURY S.
RALPH A.J.
RALPH L.W.
RATCLIFFE E.M.
RAWLING J.L.
REDDICK R.F.
REDWOOD R.
REIDY W.R.
REILLY W.J.L.
RICHARDSON J.B.
RICHARDSO L.E.
RICHMOND R.W.
RIDDOCH S.J.
RIGNEY A.M.
RIPPER W.
ROBERTS A.F.
ROBERTSON A.
ROBERTSON G.J.
ROBERTSON J.
ROBERTSON J.E.
ROBILLIARD H.J.
ROBINSON H.

VINCENT G.
ENT W.V
SH A E
DLE R.V.
HAM T
HORN F
ELING S
ER J.K.
ER J.P.
ER L.J.
WALKER S E
WALLACE R
WALLEY R.K.
WALTERS F H
WARBURTON
WARING G A
WARNE V H
WARNER A K
WARNER E

2/

ABBOTT W V
ACKLAND M
ADAMS A W
ALLATT C E
ALLEN A.
ALLEY P.J.
ANDREW H I
ANGWIN E A
APSEY W.G.
ARNOLD D N
ARTHUR J R
ASCOTT J A
AUST D.G.I.
AUSTINE A
BAIRD A C
BAKER J
BAKER W.I.
BALDWIN R
BARBER J.A.
BARKER E B
BARKO L.G.
BARRETT R
BARTON A W
BAUER F B
BAXTER R.H.
BAYLY L.J.
BEAMES R
BEECROFT R
BEGG R.W.

The **LAST POST**

The LAST POST

A ceremony of love, loss and remembrance at the Australian War Memorial

Emma Campbell

NEWSOUTH

AUSTRALIAN
WAR MEMORIAL

A NewSouth book

Published by
NewSouth Publishing
University of New South Wales Press Ltd
University of New South Wales
Sydney NSW 2052
AUSTRALIA
newsouthpublishing.com

Published in association with the Australian War Memorial

First published 2018

10 9 8 7 6 5 4 3 2 1

ISBN 9781742235783 (hardback)
        9781742248639 (ePDF)

 A catalogue record for this book is available from the National Library of Australia

Design Hugh Ford and Susanne Geppert
Cover design Hugh Ford
Printer 1010

FRONT COVER IMAGE The battalion bugler of the 2/27th Battalion plays the Last Post at sundown, as the troops disappear over the hill on their way back to camp near Hammana, Lebanon, October 1941.

010451

BACK COVER IMAGE The Eternal Flame burns constant in the Pool of Reflection in remembrance of the nation's war dead.

PAIU2015/077.16

TITLE PAGE The Last Post Ceremony for the 100th anniversary of the battle of Beersheba, 31 October 2017.

2017.4.280.10

Contents

> *'In our sleep, pain that cannot forget falls drop by drop upon the heart. And in our despair, against our will comes wisdom through the awful grace of God.'*
> Aeschylus, from *Agamemnon* 458 BC

Foreword

Charles Bean was Australia's First World War official correspondent. Subsequently appointed as the official historian, he landed with the troops on Gallipoli and stayed with them at the front through the entire war.

At Pozières, France, over six weeks in 1916 he was witness to 23 000 Australian casualties. About to become one of our 6800 dead, a mortally wounded Australian asked Bean, 'Will they remember me in Australia?'

He subsequently conceived and resolved that at its end, he would build the finest memorial and museum to these men of the Australian Imperial Force (AIF) and the nurses.

Finally, in 1948, three years after an even greater cataclysm, Charles Bean articulated the vision for the Australian War Memorial:

> *Here is their spirit, in the heart of the land they loved; and here we guard the record which they themselves made.*

We remain true to Bean's vision in a world he could not have imagined.

It is tempting, human beings that we are, to settle for the broad brushstrokes, headlines, and popular imagery of our history. Our comfortable lives breed easy indifference to individual sacrifices made out of devotion to duty, in our name, and to our country. Without care, the past can become a distant stranger.

As Australia's ambassador to Belgium, I made the journey to Ieper (Ypres), Flanders, many, many times to attend the nightly Last Post Ceremony at the Menin Gate. Gazing up to the thousands of names inscribed onto this magnificent memorial to the 'missing', I longed to be told something about just one of them.

Having arrived at the Australian War Memorial late in 2012 and standing quietly in the Commemorative Area, I thought, 'We can do this, and we will.'

In 'guarding their record', we introduced the Last Post Ceremony to the nation in April 2013.

The first story we told was that of the life and death of Private Robert Poate, killed in Afghanistan less than a year earlier. Robert's proud, young face looked out to us from the framed image of him next to the Pool of Reflection.

In the presence of his parents, family, friends, and Australia's military leadership, we gathered in awkward humility and solemnity.

The therapeutic benefit of his story 'falling drop by drop upon our hearts' was clear to those of us privileged to share the experience 'in the heart of the land *he* loved'.

We sing our national anthem often, but less often do we really reflect on its meaning. In this place, however, when we are about to remember and honour just one of them – from the Boer War to Afghanistan – the emotion wells: Australians all let us rejoice, for we are young and free.

We are free. It becomes clear to those present and watching the live broadcast, why we still have that freedom.

The emotion of the ceremony is not diminished by time, although there is a sense of 'wisdom' having come decades after a painful loss 'through the awful grace of God'.

We will never forget Roma Page.

We told the story of her late husband, Robert Page, a member of the Z Special Unit who participated in the extraordinary Jaywick raid to Singapore Harbour in 1943. They married days after his return on 1 November 1943. As a secret operative, Roma was unaware of the true nature of Bob's service. He was one of the ten beheaded by the Japanese on the second disastrous raid.

On their 70th wedding anniversary in 2013 we told Bob's Last Post story. Roma brought the flowers from their wedding cake and placed them in the wreath she laid.

Lance Corporal Luke Gavin was killed in Afghanistan in October 2011. We presented his story in the presence of his young widow, Jacky, and their three children on 10 November 2016. Also in attendance were the President of Hungary and the First Lady.

As I stood at the base of the Pool of Reflection, Jacky and her children on my left and the President's wife on my right alongside her husband, we listened to Luke's story. Gazing at his photograph, we learned of his life, his love of family and country, his army service, and his death.

I was aware of the Hungarian president's wife sobbing as the story unfolded.

At the end of the service, Luke's youngest daughter, Olivia – only six years old – pointed to the President's wife.

'Is that the president?' she asked me. I replied, 'No darling, that is his wife.'

This little girl rushed to her, wrapped her arms around her legs and looked up, saying: 'It's okay to cry. I cry about it a lot too.'

The sounding of the Last Post means more to Australia and Australians than we can ever know.

This simple gesture is undertaken with such generous dignity by the Memorial's staff and buglers. It resonates in the hearts and homes of all families whom we honour in this nightly ritual. We are able to broadcast the service live to thousands of viewers thanks to the RSL & Services Clubs Association, RSL Queensland, and RSL Victoria.

Although many dignitaries attend, this is not a ceremony for the great, the noble, and people of position.

It is an expression of loss, suffering, and love. It reaches into us all – across class, age, religion and nationality. Pausing in the cloisters and surrounds of the Pool of Reflection, stillness descends.

Visitors and pilgrims are bound by abiding reverence and a single emotion. A cloak of remembrance wraps all who gather in mourning as a reminder that we are all equal in death.

These stories instil in us a greater belief in ourselves and a deeper understanding of what it means to be *Australian*.

The Last Post, sounded from the Tomb of the Unknown Australian Soldier, arrests the soul.

The silence that surrounds it is the most powerful sound ever heard.

In that silence, I always look up to the names of young men and women on bronze panels whose lives are silent witnesses to the future they have given us. Each name and each story told reminds us of what was lost.

Those gathered from across the nation and all parts of the world – including former foes – in their reverential reflection, quietly recommit themselves to one another and the ideals of mankind.

The words of Charles Bean end the service:

Many a man lying out there at Pozières or in the low scrub at Gallipoli, with his poor tired senses barely working through the fever of his brain, has thought in his last moments – 'Well – well – it's over; but in Australia they will be proud of this.'

And we are. We are damned proud.

We are stirred by these words and emotions to remember that the most fragile yet powerful of human emotions is hope.

Visitors to the Last Post Ceremony are left inspired by fundamental twin ideals.

First, we are Australians. There are some truths by which we live that are worth fighting to defend; politically, diplomatically and, at times, militarily.

Second, sustaining precious belief in a better future, we honour them best by the way we live our lives and shape our nation.

At each ceremony the Ode is recited, taken from Laurence Binyon's *For the fallen*, first published in 1914. But also bequeathed to us in this poem is this:

Solemn the drums thrill;
Death august and royal
Sings sorrow up into immortal spheres.
There is music in the midst of desolation
And a glory that shines upon our tears.

For the music in the desolation of our mournful grieving that speaks directly to the hearts of families and people everywhere, we are honoured to offer this simple, nightly ceremony. The Last Post gives meaning where often there was none and in doing so enriches us all.

The Honourable Dr Brendan Nelson AO
Director, Australian War Memorial

Introduction

'It was a very emotional time for all of us. Dad [a Second World War veteran] started to cry after the wreathlaying, which of course triggered me off too. So many people and army officers came up to introduce themselves and shake hands with Dad after the ceremony, it was fantastic. It certainly made Dad's day being recognised for taking his part in the war.'
Vicki Curtis, attending the Last Post Ceremony of Corporal Samuel Walker, 2/4th Battalion, AIF

Every evening, people from all walks of life gather together at the Australian War Memorial for the daily Last Post Ceremony. On each occasion, the story of one person who died in war or on operational service is read by a serving member of the Australian Defence Force (ADF). Those in attendance can lay flowers or wreaths in remembrance, and the event concludes with the playing of the Last Post, a bugle call that has come to symbolise a farewell to those who died on the battlefield.

First World War official historian Charles Bean founded the Memorial to ensure that the nation would never forget the spirit of those who served, and to help others understand the battles in which they fought. Through objects, military equipment, and art, the museum tells the story of Australia's participation in conflicts and peacekeeping operations over more than a century. Individual experiences of war are not as easy to exhibit, however, or even to include in the official histories, and in most cases the stories of the men and women who served have not been formally recorded.

Beginning as the vision of Director Dr Brendan Nelson, who was inspired by the daily ceremony of the same name held at the Menin Gate Memorial to the Missing in Ypres, Belgium, the Australian War Memorial's Last Post Ceremony aims to rectify this: revealing the personal details of a serving member's life – including their childhood, family, and early pursuits – as well as their war service and manner of death. It helps visitors better understand the service and sacrifice of the more than 102 800 Australians whose names are set in bronze on the Memorial's Roll of Honour.

'These stories are one way of making our history live,' said Dr Nelson when the ceremony was introduced in 2013. 'Who was this person? Where did they grow up? What did they do and how did they die for us? We owe it to the memory of those 102 800 men and women.'[1]

LEFT An Australian Army warrant officer in a moment of reflection in the Roll of Honour cloisters, which contain the names of the 102 800 Australians who have died in war and on operational service. 2016.8.131.20

'Throughout Australia's history we have seen our young sons and daughters answer the call of their nation and willingly venture into the fray to fight for our way of life. The Last Post Ceremonies provide a very personal window into individual service, and by doing so provide us all with a much greater sense of just how much these Australians have sacrificed.' Ben Roberts-Smith VC MG

—— ● ——

Robert Poate served and died in the war in Afghanistan. On the afternoon of 17 April 2013 his story was read out at the Memorial's inaugural Last Post Ceremony. Among the hundreds gathered in the Commemorative Area were Poate's family, the Chief of the Defence Force, the four living Australian Victoria Cross recipients, a New Zealand Victoria Cross winner, friends, servicemen and servicewomen, and members of the public.

Poate's story was read by Corporal Daniel Keighran VC, a 'brother-in-arms' of the 6th Battalion, Royal Australian Regiment (6RAR), who had previously received the Victoria Cross for his actions in Afghanistan. Poate's parents and sister stood in silence as they listened to Keighran recount his fellow soldier's life, and the event of his death eight months earlier. Several of Poate's friends laid wreaths at the Pool of Reflection beside a

photograph of the grinning redhead, standing in front of a Bushmaster.

Charismatic, courageous, and funny, Poate was inspired to join the Australian Army because it resonated with the outdoor pursuits he loved, such as camping, fishing, and hunting. Born in Canberra to Hugh and Janny, he was the younger brother of Nicola and a friend to many, who called him 'Poatey'. At school he was a keen student and a superb all-round athlete; his former rugby coach said he was 'even-tempered and resourceful, with an unwavering strength of character'. He was a natural leader with a determination to succeed.

RIGHT Private Robert Poate, 6RAR. 2016.153.36
FACING PAGE The inaugural Last Post Ceremony for Private Robert Poate, 17 April 2013.
PA1U2013/052.02

ABOVE LEFT (From left to right) Australian Victoria Cross recipients Corporal Daniel Keighran, Corporal Mark Donaldson, Keith Payne, and Corporal Ben Roberts-Smith, with George Cross recipient Michael Pratt, and New Zealand Victoria Cross recipient Bill 'Willie' Apiata at the inaugural Last Post Ceremony. PAIU2013/053.12

ABOVE RIGHT Friends of Robert Poate gather around his photograph after the ceremony. PAIU2013/052.06

FACING PAGE Hugh, Nicola, and Janny Poate after laying a wreath for Robert. PAIU2013/053.03

Poate enlisted in 2009 and underwent rigorous training as an infantry soldier before being posted as a rifleman to D Company of 6RAR. D Company had a proud history of fighting at the battle of Long Tan, one of the most dramatic actions of the Vietnam War, and Poate was honoured to be part of this esteemed unit.

The young soldier joined 6RAR as it was preparing to go to war in Afghanistan, but was not included in its initial deployment with Mentoring Task Force One. Australian forces were part of the US-led international war on terror in Afghanistan from the start of operations in October 2001, and their involvement was wide-ranging. In the initial stages, the ADF provided air support and transport for coalition forces, patrols and boarding operations at sea, and ground troops for reconnaissance and the pursuit of al-Qaeda and the Taliban. Over the years, as the focus of the international commitment changed, the ADF deployed reconstruction forces to improve the Afghan people's quality of life, before a final priority shift to mentoring Afghanistan's security forces in preparation for the end of the mission.

Poate, meanwhile, was training to drive and command a Bushmaster vehicle – a sought-after skill in the desert conditions of the Middle East. In early 2012 he was told he was being sent to Afghanistan as crew commander of a Bushmaster. Delivering the news to his concerned parents, Poate said that if he didn't go, 'it would be like training for three-and-a-half years in a football team and not getting a run on the field'.

He arrived in Afghanistan in June 2012, when the ADF was nearing the end of its most intense phase of mentoring with the Afghan National Army and the Afghan National Police. During this period, Australian forces had been expected to not only train their Afghan counterparts but also accompany them on patrols and engage with insurgents. They lived together on patrol bases scattered throughout Uruzgan province and, for the Australians, this meant navigating cultural differences and customs.

Poate's Bushmaster was routinely the lead vehicle in convoys and patrols undertaken by the Australians – a testament to his skills and his senior colleagues' confidence in him. On the night of 29 August 2012, Poate and a small group of Australian soldiers were relaxing at Patrol Base Wahab when a rogue Afghan soldier fired on them without warning. Poate was killed in the insider attack, along with Lance Corporal Stjepan 'Rick' Milosevic and Sapper James Martin. Two of their comrades were wounded.

Private Robert Poate – a dedicated soldier, a larrikin, and a great mate – was 23.

'Despite the efforts of all those who served in conflicts from 1914 to today, and particularly those who paid the ultimate sacrifice, world peace remains as elusive as ever. The 102 800 names on the Roll of Honour are a reminder of the terrible human cost of war. We must never forget.'

Hugh Poate, father of Private Robert Poate, to whom the inaugural Last Post Ceremony was dedicated

'The ceremony for my uncle, Thomas Fryer, meant a great deal to the members of my family who were able to attend and to many who weren't ... I was very moved by the dignity of the occasion and the clear focus placed on that one soldier.'
Rosalie Richards, niece of Lance Corporal Thomas Edward Fryer, 54th Battalion, AIF

Since its introduction, the Last Post Ceremony has become one of the Memorial's most popular public events. More than one million people visit the site annually, and many stay especially to attend the late afternoon ceremony. Heads of state, international dignitaries, military chiefs, war veterans, national sporting teams, families of the fallen, and school children stand side-by-side with members of the public to remember and reflect upon the lives ended by conflict.

Hundreds of people have requested that Last Post Ceremonies be arranged for family members or ancestors, and many have travelled interstate or from overseas to attend. Other individuals are chosen for remembrance in a ceremony because of their connection to a significant action, unit, or group, particularly when commemorating a military anniversary. Sometimes the story of a serviceman or servicewoman is uncovered during historical research. The ceremony is streamed live, so that people across Australia and the world can participate. It has even been adopted by other museums and memorials in countries like New Zealand and the United States.

LEFT Last Post Ceremonies are among the Memorial's most important commemorative events. PAIU2013/154.34
ABOVE Visitors of all ages and backgrounds attend Last Post Ceremonies. 2016.8.133.1

'Thank you. You are all doing such a wonderful and valuable job, bringing lots of families together.'
Marg Quodling, descendant of Private Granville Clarke, 55th Battalion, AIF

This book tells the story of the Last Post Ceremony and how, through the dedicated endeavour of Memorial staff, it has become a significant part of Australia's remembrance program. In that same spirit, it features a selection of the personal stories of individual service and sacrifice that have formed the focus of the ceremony since that first commemoration of the life and death of Private Robert Poate. Each ceremony is unique, and the photographs contained within this volume are a poignant reflection of the moving, thoughtful, amusing, and human moments that occur at each one. Accompanied by the words of those who have requested, researched, participated in, attended, or hosted a Last Post Ceremony, the following pages showcase the involvement of hundreds of people, from Memorial staff to Australian families, the ADF, the Returned and Services League, veterans, school groups, and the broader community.

The book also explores why Australians commemorate war, and how we have done so since Federation in 1901, revealing the central role that the Australian War Memorial plays in our national story.

It will take nearly 300 years for the Last Post Ceremony to commemorate every person currently on the Roll of Honour. The Memorial is committed to ensuring that each story of a life lived and a person loved will eventually be told.

ABOVE The Last Post Ceremony's purpose is to help visitors better understand the service and sacrifice of the more than 102 800 Australians whose names are set in bronze on the Memorial's Roll of Honour. 2016.8.154.8

FACING PAGE LEFT The distinctive copper dome of the Australian War Memorial. PAIU2013/052.14

FACING PAGE RIGHT The Memorial plays a central role in national commemoration. 2017.4.185.14

Private Thomas Anderson Whyte, 10th Battalion, Australian Imperial Force

Died of wounds: 25 April 1915

Thomas Anderson Whyte, known as 'Tom' to his family and friends, was born in the Adelaide suburb of Unley. He attended St Peter's Anglican College in Adelaide, and served for three years in a local infantry Militia. He became a prominent sportsman, and while he played a number of interstate lacrosse matches for South Australia between 1908 and 1912, he was best known as a rower. He rowed for the Mercantile Rowing Club in 1903 and developed into a particularly successful crew member. He represented South Australia in team events across the country and became a popular member of the Adelaide Rowing Club. It was reported that there was 'no doubt that Tom Whyte was one of the best oarsmen South Australia ever produced'.

In 1912 Whyte became engaged to Eileen Wallace Champion, whom he said he loved more than he felt it was possible for a man to love.

Whyte enlisted in the Australian Imperial Force within weeks of the outbreak of the First World War in 1914. He was posted to A Company of the 10th Battalion, along with many of his mates from the Adelaide Rowing Club. He left Adelaide in October and travelled to Egypt for further training. There he participated in rowing races when possible and enjoyed joking with his mates.

Whyte rowed one of the first boats ashore on Gallipoli on 25 April 1915. The job of rowing was a dangerous one, as the oarsmen were especially exposed to enemy fire. Nevertheless,

according to his friend Arthur Blackburn, Whyte 'was laughing and joking all the way to the shore'. As the boat pulled up on the shingle, however, Whyte slipped over to the side. He had been seriously wounded by a gunshot wound through the pelvis and was evacuated to a hospital ship for immediate treatment.

The day before the landings, Whyte had written to his fiancée:

I can't realise myself how thoughts of you have completely obsessed every waking minute for the past month. Every step, every action has been preceded by the thought, 'How will this strike Eileen'. Oh god, I love you. As this is only intended to reach you in the event of my death, you will know that my thoughts will have been of you right until the end. Of this I feel absolutely certain. You can't imagine how it hurts to write this letter. The one thing I can't bear to think of is the possibility of not being able to see you, to marry you, to live the happiest of lives with you.

ABOVE Whyte's fiancée, Eileen Wallace Champion. P09576.001
RIGHT A framed photograph of Whyte belonging to Champion. REL42616
LEFT Private Thomas 'Tom' Whyte (left) and Sergeant John Gordon on the Great Pyramid at Giza, c. December 1914 to April 1915. P09576.002

On the night of 25 April 1915, Whyte died from his wounds aboard the hospital ship *Gascon*. He was 29 years old.

He was buried at sea, and his name is listed on the Lone Pine Memorial on Gallipoli, among nearly 5000 Anzac soldiers who have no known grave.

Dr Meleah Hampton

Sister Mary Eleanor McGlade, 113th Australian General Hospital, Australian Army Nursing Service, Second Australian Imperial Force

Executed: 16 February 1942

Sister Mary 'Ellie' McGlade at the time of her enlistment. P02785.002

Mary Eleanor McGlade was born on 2 July 1902 in Armidale, New South Wales, to Francis Aloysius and Agnes Beatrice McGlade. Her mother died shortly after her birth, and her father followed in 1905. 'Ellie' was taken in by her aunt, Mrs Walter Scott.

From a young age McGlade attended St Ursula's Convent in Armidale as a boarder. At first she slept in a cot beside Mother Berchman's bed, and as she grew, the convent became a beloved childhood home. She won prizes at school for singing, violin, piano, and Christian doctrine, and completed her Intermediate Certificate in 1920. By this time, she had already begun to care for girls who fell ill. The School Report of 1921 noted:

Owing to the kind solicitude of their College Infirmarian no one has a chance to get seriously ill before she is reported and nursed back to normal by the indefatigable Ellie.

On leaving school McGlade visited relatives in Scotland and Ireland, returning to begin training as a nurse at the Royal Prince Alfred Hospital in Sydney. Graduating in 1927 with certificates in General Nursing, Cooking, and Dispensing, she became a Mothercraft Nurse in the Hunter Valley.

The outbreak of the Second World War in September 1939 led hundreds of thousands of Australians to volunteer for active duty, and in January 1941 McGlade enlisted in the Australian Army Nursing Service. Called up that August and appointed to the 2/13th Australian General Hospital (AGH), she embarked for Singapore on the hospital ship *Wanganella*, arriving in September. Here she worked with the 13th AGH in Tampoi, near Johore.

The Japanese attacked Pearl Harbor in December 1941, and invaded a number of countries in the Asia–Pacific region, including Thailand, Hong Kong, the Philippines, New Guinea, Malaya, and the Solomon Islands. Allied forces in Singapore attempted to resist the Japanese, but were ultimately forced to surrender on 15 February 1942. The 13th AGH, which had remained operational during much of the battle, evacuated its personnel three days before the fall. McGlade was one of 65 Australian nurses who left Singapore aboard the *Vyner Brooke*, but two days later the Japanese bombed the ship and many lives were lost. Those who could swim made for nearby Banka Island.

Some of the survivors travelled to the nearest port to formally surrender to the Japanese, but McGlade was among 22 Australian nurses who remained on the beach to tend the wounded.

On the morning of 16 February a group of Japanese soldiers arrived and ordered the wounded men around a headland, where they were subsequently killed.

Back on the beach, the remaining survivors were ordered to walk into the sea. When the water reached their waists the Japanese opened fire with machine-guns. Of the Australian nurses ordered into the sea, all but one were killed, including Ellie McGlade. She was 39 years old.

Back home in Armidale, a requiem mass was held for her in St Ursula's Convent chapel.

Christina Zissis

Lieutenant Colonel Charles Hercules Green DSO, 3rd Battalion, Royal Australian Regiment, Australian Army

Died of wounds: 1 November 1950

Charles 'Charlie' Green served in the Second World War and in the Korean War. P02037.024

Charles Hercules Green was born on 26 December 1919 in Grafton, New South Wales. He left school at age 13 to take up farming on his parents' property and, at 16, he joined the 41st Battalion in his local Militia unit. He was soon promoted to sergeant and in 1939 was commissioned as a second lieutenant.

When the Second World War began in September, Green volunteered for service on the first day that recruiting centres opened. He was commissioned as a lieutenant into the 2/2nd Battalion, Australian Imperial Force. On his final leave, Green had a fateful encounter at his local newsagents when he bought a fountain pen from the store-owner's daughter, Olwyn Warner.

Green's unit left for the Middle East, where treatment for a septic foot caused him to miss the battalion's first actions at Bardia and Tobruk. He took part in the ill-fated campaign in Greece when, during the Allied retreat, Green and several comrades were separated from the battalion and made a daring escape, eventually reuniting with their battered comrades in Palestine.

After this, Green began to write to Olwyn with the fountain pen he had carried with him through the Middle East and Greece. From then on they exchanged frequent letters.

Returning to Australia in August 1942, Green was promoted to major, and in January 1943 he and Olwyn were married. He spent much of the next two years as an infantry instructor, and underwent senior officer training. He was posted to New Guinea in December 1944 and the following March, aged 25, he took charge of the 2/11th Battalion as the youngest Australian to command a battalion during the Second World War. He was awarded the Distinguished Service Order for his leadership during the Wewak campaign.

Green returned to Grafton after the war and soon his daughter, Anthea, was born. In 1948 he was promoted to lieutenant colonel and given command of the 41st Battalion, Citizen Military Forces. With the establishment of the Australian Regular Army in 1949, Green returned to full-time service and attended the staff college at Queenscliff, Victoria.

When the 3rd Battalion, Royal Australian Regiment (3RAR), was committed to the Korean War in September 1950, Green was sent to Japan to take command. He had two weeks to weld his men into a cohesive unit before being deployed to the main theatre of war. In late October, Green successfully led 3RAR through its first battles at Yongju (known as the Apple Orchard), Kujin, and Chongju.

In the evening of 30 October, 3RAR was fired on by North Korean artillery and Charlie Green, who was resting in his tent, was hit in the stomach by shrapnel. He was evacuated to a nearby hospital but died on 1 November 1950. He was 31 years old.

Michael Kelly

Lieutenant Anthony Austin Casadio, Royal Australian Navy Helicopter Flight Vietnam, Royal Australian Navy

Helicopter crash: 21 August 1968

Known as 'Tony' to his friends and family, Anthony Casadio was born in Port Lincoln in South Australia on 30 December 1945. He grew up in Mount Gambier, where he attended Marist Brothers College.

Casadio joined the Royal Australian Navy (RAN) in 1964 and trained as a helicopter pilot. After graduating in 1966 as an acting sub-lieutenant from the Royal Australian Air Force flying school at Pearce in Western Australia, he began flying helicopters from HMAS *Melbourne*.

In 1967 his rank of sub-lieutenant was confirmed, and he joined the first contingent of the RAN Helicopter Flight Vietnam, which had been formed to support US and South Vietnamese ground forces. The Australians fully integrated into the US Army 135th Assault Helicopter Company. Known as EMU – the Experimental Military Unit – the unit took on the large flightless bird as an ironic mascot and call sign. The motto of the company also had a typically Australian ring to it: 'Get the bloody job done.'

The 135th Assault Helicopter Company flew US Army Iroquois 'Huey' helicopters in two configurations: the gunship and the troop transport or 'slick'. Casadio was a gunship pilot, and the pilot of the first helicopter of the unit to be shot down.

On 19 November 1967 Casadio was piloting a helicopter attacking a Viet Cong position when his gunship's fuel tanks were punctured by small-arms fire. He managed to successfully crash-land the aircraft in enemy-controlled territory in the Rung Sat Special Zone near Saigon. Then, using the helicopter's machine-guns, he and the gunship crew were able to hold off advancing Viet Cong soldiers before being rescued by another EMU helicopter. For his leadership, skill, and courage during this encounter, Casadio was awarded the US Distinguished Flying Cross – the first gallantry award to be won by a naval aviator in Vietnam.

In December 1967 the company moved from the increasingly crowded base at Vung Tau to the US Fire Support Base Black Horse near Xuan Loc. From there the unit flew troop lift, combat assault, and support missions in Phuoc Tuy province and the Mekong Delta. The helicopters often came under heavy fire while inserting and extracting US, Australian, and South Vietnamese soldiers. In early 1968, Casadio was promoted to the rank of lieutenant.

On 21 August 1968 Casadio was leading a team of gunships, flying at tree-top level from Black Horse to Nui Dat, when his gunship was struck by a rocket-propelled grenade. He crashed in a clearing and Casadio, fellow Australian Petty Officer O'Brian Phillips, and two American crew members were killed on impact.

The loss of the four men was keenly felt at Black Horse base, all the more because Casadio was ten months into his 12-month tour of duty. A memorial service was held in the days after the incident. Casadio's record of 'constant heroic acts and exceptional devotion to duty' was posthumously Mentioned in Despatches. He was 22 years old. His remains were transported home, and buried in the Carinya Gardens Cemetery in Mount Gambier.

Dr Thomas Rogers

Lieutenant Anthony 'Tony' Casadio (left) performs a pre-flight check on his Iroquois helicopter, assisted by Leading Airman Weapons Arthur Burton, 1967.

NAVY15002

Chapter one
The origins of the Last Post

RIGHT A bugler sounds the Last Post at the conclusion of the Last Post Ceremony. PAIU2013/044.04
FOLLOWING PAGES Visitors to the Memorial, including dignitaries, members of the Australian Defence Force and school children, are silent and respectful during the playing of the Last Post. 2017.4.242.34

When a bugler sounds the Last Post, we listen and remember. The poignant tune evokes memories of men and women who have performed great deeds, led others with integrity, and died for their country. The sparsely played notes – powerful, sombre, elegant – convey a genuine sense of loss.

The Last Post is well-known today in Commonwealth nations as a commemorative anthem for war dead, and in Australia it has traditionally been a feature of ceremonies held on Anzac Day and Remembrance Day. It has a more practical origin, however, as one of a number of traditional bugle calls used by the military to mark the phases of the day.

Bugles, horns, and drums have been used since Roman times as signals to command soldiers on the battlefield and to regulate camp life. Men would be roused from sleep by Reveille, and further daily activities would be prompted by other beats or calls.

From the beginning of the seventeenth century, the British Army had an elaborate evening routine known as the 'tattoo'. This was drawn from an older Dutch custom, 'doe den tap toe', a signal sounded in the towns to indicate that beer taps had to be shut off for the night. In the army, the routine was originally set to drums, but later incorporated bugle horns. As daylight fell, an officer would do the rounds of his unit's position to check that the sentry posts were manned, and round up the off-duty soldiers and send them to their billets. Accompanying the officer would be one or more musicians. The 'first post' bugle call was sounded when the inspection began and a drum was played as the party went from post to post. The drumbeats told off-duty soldiers it was time to rest and, if the soldiers were in a town, it prompted them to leave the taverns.

When the officer completed his rounds and reached the 'last post', another bugle call was sounded to signal that the night sentries were alert at their posts, and give one last warning to the other soldiers: the day's activities were at an end and the barracks were closed. A final and brief sounding, for 'lights out', was played 15 to 30 minutes later.

In the 1850s, the Last Post bugle call was incorporated into military funerals as a final farewell, signifying that the duty of the dead was over and they could rest in peace. The music evolved its commemorative function after the Boer War of 1899–1902, coinciding with an increase in the erection of war memorials in Britain. The bugle call was played at the unveiling ceremonies, raising its status to a refrain of remembrance.[2]

In Australia, the term 'Last Post' was being used in newspapers at the turn of the twentieth century in connection with men who died in the Boer War, and was played at the unveiling of some of the memorials erected to that conflict. It became more widely known, however, after the end of the First World War.

At the first Remembrance Day commemoration in 1919, on the anniversary of the Armistice that ended the war, the Last Post was played at ceremonies held in cities across Australia. The key part of the formalities was a two-minute silence, which King George V had proclaimed should be observed at the 11th hour of the 11th day of the 11th month. The *Age* newspaper reported that at the Remembrance Day event held outside the nation's parliament (then situated in Melbourne) 'all heads were immediately uncovered, and for the ensuing two minutes there was not a sound to be heard ... when the solemn notes of the Last Post were sounded by the buglers at the termination of the period of silence there were hundreds of tear-dimmed eyes'.[3]

In the years that followed, the Last Post became a feature of public commemoration that accorded with the construction and dedication of hundreds more war memorials in towns and cities across the nation. On Anzac Day – the anniversary of the Gallipoli landings of 25 April 1915, which was officially established as a national day of commemoration during the 1920s – the Dawn Service included a lone bugler playing the Last Post, followed by a period of silence, which concluded with Reveille.

The playing of the Last Post at the inauguration of the Menin Gate Memorial to the Missing in the Belgian city of Ypres in July 1927 made a strong impression on many of those who attended.

LEFT Buglers from Ypres' Last Post Association have performed at the Memorial's ceremonies. PA1U2014/049.18
RIGHT Crowds fill the city streets in Melbourne on Armistice Day, 11 November 1918. J00348

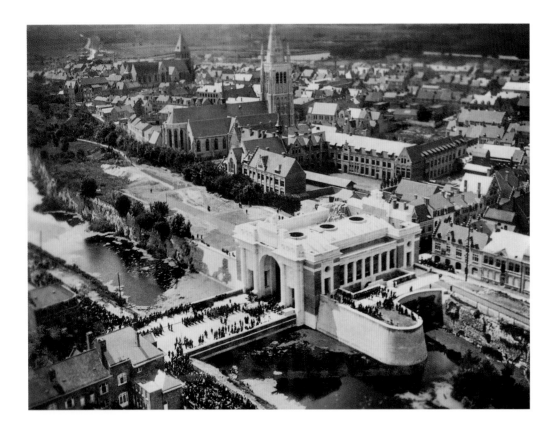

The elegant stone arch was built by the British to commemorate those from Australia, Canada, India, South Africa, and the United Kingdom who were killed in the Ypres Salient – a much-contested battleground in Belgian Flanders – but had no known grave. The site was symbolic: during the First World War hundreds of thousands of troops passed through the old wall defences on the Menin Road as they headed towards the front line. The memorial to the missing bears the names of more than 54 000 men, including almost 6200 men of the Australian Imperial Force.

The local commissioner of police, Pierre Vandenbraambussche, was part of the ensuing community conversation as to how the city of Ypres could continue to show its gratitude and respect to those who had served and died in the region.[4]

LEFT The Menin Gate Memorial, with the city of Ypres beyond. H15967
RIGHT The official unveiling of the Menin Gate Memorial to the Missing in Ypres, Belgium, on 24 July 1927. H16916

ABOVE Troops march toward the Menin Gate at Ypres on 28 September 1917. E04678

LEFT The ruins of the Cloth Hall on the road leading to the Menin Gate in October 1917. E01126

Artist Will Longstaff painted *Menin Gate at midnight* after attending the Menin Gate Memorial's inauguration ceremony in 1927. The painting has attained an iconic status and is part of the Memorial's collection.

LEFT Last Post Association bugler
Dirk Vandekerckhove at a Last Post
Ceremony in 2014. PAIU2014/049.14
RIGHT An officer pauses to read a
card on a floral tribute following
a Last Post Ceremony. 2017.4.127.32

The year after the memorial's unveiling, Vandenbraambussche began a tradition that continues to this day:[5] every night at eight o'clock a bugler sounds the Last Post beneath the memorial's arch. Traffic is halted for the occasion, which can attract thousands of visitors. It is a simple but powerful act of remembrance of the soldiers of the British Empire who died in the Great War, held by the descendants of those whose land they fought to protect. The ceremony also commemorates Britain's 'comrades-in-arms' from Belgium, France, and other allied nations.[6]

In the years since the First World War, the Last Post has become, as cultural historian Alwyn W. Turner notes, an 'almost sacred anthem in an increasingly secular society'.[7] While it has been mostly associated with war commemoration, it has also been used beyond

military events and the funerals of those who have served. In 1948 the Last Post was sounded at the funeral of Mahatma Gandhi, the leader of India's independence movement, and it was also played at the burial service for former President of South Africa Nelson Mandela in 2013.

Turner has also observed a change to the bugle call over the years:

Notes are held for longer, the pauses extended, the expression more mournful, so that it now lasts around 75 seconds, rather than the 45 seconds it used to take to mark the end of the day. And it has been infused by a mass of memories and memorials, so that what was once jaunty is now simply sorrowful.[8]

LEFT The public has embraced the daily Last Post Ceremony, which concludes with the playing of the Last Post. 2017.4.127

RIGHT School children often participate in ceremonies. 2017.4.197.2

Today the Last Post is played at commemorative events and military funerals in various Commonwealth nations, including Canada, South Africa, and New Zealand. Equivalent pieces of music are played at remembrance events in other countries: in Italy, they play 'Il silenzio' (The silence); the Spanish Armed Forces have adopted the hymn 'La muerte no es el final' (Death is not the end); and the French Armed Forces commemorate with 'La sonnerie aux morts' (The call to the dead). Probably the most well-known equivalent is the bugle call of the US Armed Forces, 'Taps', whose name is also derived from the Dutch term 'taptoe'.[9]

In 2013 Director Dr Brendan Nelson named the Memorial's daily closing service the 'Last Post Ceremony'. The bugle call is played at the conclusion of the ceremony as a paean to the courage and selflessness of the servicemen and servicewomen who have fought and died for Australia over more than a century.

'The playing of the Last Post always affects me profoundly,' said Dr Nelson at the time. 'I want to ensure that the ceremony that ends the day at the Memorial is remembered by all those who visit this great institution.'[10]

Warrant Officer Class 1 Gordon Wallace Duff, 2/3rd Battalion, Second Australian Imperial Force

Killed in action: 24 October 1942

Gordon 'Bill' Duff served in the Middle East, Greece, and on the Kokoda Trail in New Guinea.

Image courtesy of the Duff family.

Gordon Duff was born on 15 February 1915 in the western Sydney suburb of Auburn, one of six children of Alexander and Rose Duff. He was known to friends and family as 'Bill'. His father worked for many years for the Department of Railways in Sydney and around New South Wales. He was the stationmaster at Kempsey on the state's north coast, and then at Corrimal on the south coast.

When the Second World War broke out in September 1939, Gordon Duff was 24 years old, working as a labourer, and living with his family in the station residence at Corrimal. He volunteered for the Second Australian Imperial Force (AIF) on 20 October and joined the 2/3rd Battalion, which was part of the newly raised 6th Division. In January 1940 the division sailed for the Middle East. After a year of hard training, it spearheaded the British advance from Egypt into Libya in January 1941, capturing the Italian fortresses of Bardia and Tobruk. Duff was promoted to acting corporal in July 1940 and acting sergeant in January 1941.

In March 1941 the 6th Division moved to Greece, where it joined the New Zealand division and British troops. German troops invaded Greece in early April, forcing the Commonwealth and Greek defenders to withdraw. The 2/3rd Battalion was heavily involved in the blocking action at Tempe Gorge (or Pinios) on 18 April, but the Commonwealth's campaign ended a week later in defeat and evacuation.

In June and July the main body of the 2/3rd Battalion fought against the Vichy French in Lebanon during the Syrian campaign. Around Damascus it took part in an unsuccessful effort to secure Jebel Mazar, as well as in the climactic battle of Damour. After participating in these three campaigns, Duff was an experienced combat veteran. He continued to be promoted regularly, and by the end of the year was a warrant officer class 1.

In 1942 the 6th Division and other elements of the AIF began returning to Australia to face a new enemy – the Japanese. On the way home, the 2/3rd Battalion spent close to three months as part of the force garrisoning Ceylon (present-day Sri Lanka).

The battalion returned home in August, but its time on Australian soil was fleeting. Because of the worsening crisis in Papua – where the Japanese were pushing along the Kokoda Trail – elements of the 6th Division, including the 2/3rd Battalion, were sent to Port Moresby in September. With little time to acclimatise, the battalion reinforced the Australian advance along the Kokoda Trail. From 22 October it became involved in a major action at Eora Creek, and fierce fighting continued for days. On 24 October, as Duff was carrying ammunition to a forward company, he was shot and killed by a group of five Japanese soldiers.

Duff was 27 years old. He was subsequently Mentioned in Despatches, and is buried in Bomana War Cemetery at Port Moresby. The epitaph engraved on this tombstone reads simply, 'His duty nobly done'.

Dr Karl James

Lieutenant Stanley Spencer Reid, 6th Western Australian Mounted Infantry, Colonial Military Forces

Died of wounds: 29 June 1901

RIGHT Lieutenant Stanley Reid's name on the Boer War panel of the Roll of Honour. 2017.4.278.11

Stanley Spencer Reid was born on 12 July 1872 in Swan Hill, Victoria, the oldest of seven children of Sybil and the Reverend John Bentley Reid, a respected minister of the Presbyterian Church. Stanley was educated at Scotch College in Melbourne and went on to study arts at Melbourne University, where he was voted one of the best all-round athletes of his time. He was an Australian Rules footballer for the Fitzroy Football Club from 1894 to 1898. He also played cricket, and competed in running, boxing, tennis, shooting, and riding.

After university Reid entered the ministry and graduated from his theological course at Ormond College in October 1898. His first church was St George's Presbyterian Church in Boulder, Western Australia, where he began working in December 1898. He was a great favourite both within his congregation and outside of it.

When the call went out for Australian contingents to the Boer War in 1899, Stanley Reid attempted to enlist as a chaplain. He was unsuccessful, and instead enlisted as a trooper in the 2nd Western Australian Mounted Infantry. At his farewell function he said he 'hoped they would be able to say they had given a farewell to a man who had taken his part for the British Empire'. He served in South Africa for most of 1900, mainly patrolling for small groups of Boers. In August, as the Western Australians participated in a general advance from Pretoria, Trooper Reid and another man were separated from the column and went missing for about 16 days.

According to Reid's account they stumbled onto a Boer stronghold and were nearly trapped, but managed to escape and rejoin the unit. Reid was known as an excellent soldier who 'simply did not know what fear was … his bravery was of a reckless, dashing kind'. His courage saw him Mentioned in Despatches by General Kitchener.

Reid returned to Australia with his contingent towards the end of 1900, but by early 1901 he was back in South Africa, this time as a lieutenant with the 6th Western Australian Mounted Infantry. His brother Francis had also offered his services as a doctor and was stationed nearby.

That June the 5th and 6th Western Australian Mounted Infantry left camp near Middelburg and advanced towards some Boer positions. Lieutenant Reid took some men forward 'to see what was over the sky-line'. Those left behind heard a heavy burst of continuous fire and, as they watched, a group of Boers chased two of Reid's men back over a ridge. The enemy were repelled, and Reid and his group were found with two dead and three wounded, including Lieutenant Reid, shot through the stomach.

Reid was taken back to camp. His brother stayed near him the whole time, but the case was hopeless. He died on 29 June 1901, aged 29. Francis later wrote: 'The men of the contingent fairly worshipped him, and are very cut up over his death.'

Dr Meleah Hampton

PAGE F.
PARKER W.
REID S.S.
SEMPLE J.
SOLOMON H.
SPENCER R. W

Lieutenant Robert David Burns,
14th Australian Machine Gun Company,
Australian Imperial Force

Killed in action: 20 July 1916

ABOVE Lieutenant Robert Burns
was killed at Fromelles. P08624.018
LEFT Lieutenant Burns (far right)
with fellow soldiers outside a
dug-out on Gallipoli. P01309.013

Robert Burns was born on 6 April 1888 in the Sydney suburb of Potts Point, the youngest son of Colonel Sir James and Mary Burns. His father was a Scottish emigrant who had started out working as a jackeroo in Queensland, and became the chairman of directors at Burns Philp & Co., one of the biggest trading companies in the Pacific. He was also the former commander of the New South Wales Lancers, the Militia unit that would become the 1st Australian Light Horse Brigade.

Robert Burns was working as a station manager at Gowan Brae, near Parramatta, when war was declared. He enlisted in the Australian Imperial Force (AIF) in May 1915. After training with the 4th Light Horse Brigade in Australia and Egypt, that August he embarked for the fighting on Gallipoli. There he endured the hardships of the war of attrition in increasingly cold and wet conditions until the evacuation in December.

In early 1916 the AIF expanded and reorganised in preparation for the war in Europe. Burns underwent machine-gun training and was transferred through a number of units before joining the 14th Machine Gun Company. In June he left for the fighting on the Western Front.

After less than a month in France, Burns took part in Australia's first major engagement on the Western Front: the battle of Fromelles. The attack began at 6 pm on 19 July, after a seven-hour bombardment that removed any hope of surprise and which ultimately proved ineffective. While Australian troops on the left flank successfully captured German trenches, those on the right suffered devastating losses. The 5th Australian Division suffered more than 5500 casualties.

That night Burns advanced into no-man's land with the fourth wave of infantry attacks. He was seen alive the next morning, slightly wounded but still fighting. Despite being ordered to withdraw, he opted to fight on and assist other machine-gun teams. When he became surrounded, he destroyed his machine-gun to ensure it did not fall into German hands, and attempted to lead his team back to the Australian lines. He was never seen again.

Burns was originally listed as missing in action. It wasn't until March 1917 that his family received confirmation that he had been killed, aged 28. After receiving Robert's identity disc through the Red Cross, James Burns devoted great energy to discovering the fate and final resting place of his son. Despite his power and influence, his search was unsuccessful, and Robert Burns's name was listed on the Australian National Memorial at Villers-Bretonneux, among 10700 other Australians who died in France but have no known grave.

In 2008 Australian researchers located a mass grave containing the remains of 250 British and Australian soldiers near the Fromelles battleground. Burns's body was one of those identified and it was reinterred in the Fromelles (Pheasant Wood) Cemetery. The long search, started by his father decades before, was finally ended, and the headstone on Robert's grave now reads: 'Remembered with pride'.

David Sutton

Lance Corporal Shannon McAliney, 1st Battalion, Royal Australian Regiment, Australian Army

Accidentally killed: 2 April 1993

Shannon 'Mac' McAliney was born in Forbes on 8 May 1971, the only child of Liz Hanns and Michael McAliney. He attended Forbes North Public School before moving at the age of ten to Ballina, on the New South Wales north coast. He played soccer and cricket and enjoyed surfing, but from a very young age his focus was on army toys. He often expressed his desire to one day join the army and serve his country.

In 1988 Shannon left school to enlist in the Australian Regular Army. After basic training at the Recruit Training Centre in Kapooka and the Infantry Centre in Singleton he was posted to the 1st Battalion, Royal Australian Regiment (1RAR).

McAliney proved a competent and well-liked soldier, his sense of humour and willingness to work for the team endearing him to his peers and his supervisors. At the end of 1992 his enthusiasm and hard work saw him promoted to lance corporal. He also received the prestigious award of Champion Soldier of Delta Company.

That year 1RAR was chosen to deploy to Somalia as part of Australia's commitment to the US-led Unified Task Force. Its mission was to provide protection for the delivery of humanitarian aid in a country shattered by years of civil war and famine. At the time this was Australia's largest ever commitment to international peacekeeping, and the first operational service deployment by an Australian battalion group since the Vietnam War.

McAliney, like many of his mates in 1RAR, was excited by the prospect of putting his skills to the test in a real operational environment. The Australians patrolled Baidoa and the surrounding countryside, providing protection for the numerous non-government aid organisations working there. Despite the often long and gruelling hours on patrol and the inherent danger in the task, McAliney loved being in the thick of the action.

On 2 April 1993 McAliney was leading a routine night patrol in Baidoa township. As they were about to begin one of the patrol members accidentally discharged his rifle, and McAliney was shot in the chest at point-blank range. Despite immediate first aid, he died soon after arriving at the treatment camp at Baidoa airfield.

McAliney was buried with a full military funeral in his hometown of Forbes, where people remembered a mate with a good sense of humour, a courteous and polite young man, and a dutiful son. His death was a tragedy, but he had often told his mother that if he could make a difference in people's lives then his own would have been worthwhile.

The Somali woman pictured opposite alongside Mac later sent a message to his mother expressing her sympathy and describing how, for her at least, the young soldier had made a difference.

Shannon McAliney was 21 years old.

Dr Steven Bullard

Lance Corporal Shannon 'Mac' McAliney assists a Somali woman at a food distribution centre in southern Somalia during Operation Solace, March 1993. MSU/93/0179/35

Chapter two

The Australian War Memorial

*'Here is their spirit, in the heart of the land they loved;
and here we guard the record which they themselves made.'*
Charles Bean, 1948

The foundations of the Australian War Memorial were laid in the fields of France. In July and August 1916 Australian divisions were employed in bitter and costly actions in and around Pozières, a small village on the Somme. In six weeks of shelling and skirmish, 23 000 Australians were killed, wounded, or missing. The battle for Pozières was the most intense fighting experienced by the Australian Imperial Force (AIF) so far; even for Gallipoli veterans it was a distinctly horrifying and brutal campaign.

Charles Bean, Australia's official war correspondent, recorded the experiences of the soldiers from the moment they embarked for overseas service in late 1914. After witnessing the carnage at Pozières, he wrote in his diary that the area was 'more densely sown with Australian sacrifice than any other place on earth'. There and then he resolved to make plans for a national memorial to commemorate those who had served in the Great War.

Bean did not envisage a simple monument; he believed this memorial should comprise a shrine to the soldiers' memory, along with a museum and archive that would demonstrate the endurance

RIGHT The main street of Pozières following the fighting in 1916. A05776
BELOW The shattered village of Pozières in August 1916. EZ0097

'The Last Post Ceremony project is not just an exercise in understanding the lives of the soldiers and their experience; this project has really opened a window into the day-to-day lives of ordinary Australians. It has been incredibly rewarding to take a name from the Roll of Honour and discover the life and character of that person.'

Dr Meleah Hampton, Historian

and achievements of those who had served while helping Australians better understand the experience of war. Bean wanted the memorial's collection to include 'the things our men and units have actually used in battle, or which the German has used against them'.[11] These included objects, or 'relics' such as tanks and artillery pieces, weapons, tools, flags, and spent shells. He also sought the inclusion of official and private records, including military orders, maps, photographs, works of art, and letters and diaries of serving men and women – 'even those humorous incidents which are a flashlight on the character of the Australian soldier'.[12]

The AIF established the Australian War Records Section (AWRS) in London in May 1917 to make collecting an official enterprise. John Treloar, a young Australian officer, was given charge of the section. He encouraged soldiers to submit objects to the AWRS that they had taken from the battlefield, and urged fellow officers to keep detailed unit diaries. Over the next two years, the AWRS collected approximately 25 000 objects and maintained a strong assemblage of official records, which were shipped to Australia in 1919.[13]

ABOVE Official correspondent Charles Bean at Flêtre in northern France, 1917. E01429
LEFT In 1917 these grave markers littered the battlefield of Pozières. E00997

PERSPECTIVE DRAWING OF
AUSTRALIAN WAR MEMORIAL
TO BE ERECTED AT CANBERRA

At home, the impetus for a national war memorial was strong, and in the postwar years long-running exhibitions of collected items attracted large crowds in Sydney and Melbourne. But the building process in Canberra was hampered by budget difficulties and delays in design, and Bean's vision was not realised until 1941, more than two decades after the First World War ended. When the Australian War Memorial opened on Remembrance Day that year, hundreds of thousands of Australian men and women were already engaged in the Second World War.

Treloar was appointed the director of the Australian War Museum (later Memorial) in 1920, and he remained in the position for the rest of his life (apart from a brief period in charge of the Military History and Information Section during the Second World War). Bean continued his involvement with the museum, and was made chairman of its board in 1952.

ABOVE The completed joint architectural design for the Memorial, circa 1927, by Emil Sodersteen and John Crust.
XS0002

LEFT Lieutenant John Treloar, on receiving his commission in the Australian Flying Corps, March 1916.
P04505.002

RIGHT An aerial view of the official opening ceremony of the Memorial on 11 November 1941.
XS0190

'The Last Post Ceremony is one of my favourite times at the War Memorial. It has brought back the intimacy of family being able to honour their fallen and echoes the feel of the earlier dawn services at the Memorial where people gathered around the pool, embraced by the surrounding walls yet under an open sky. Safe, secure, and eternal.'

Jenny Wardrobe, visitor to the Memorial

In the decades since it opened, the Australian War Memorial has expanded in size and in scope, earning many plaudits for its world-class museum, comprehensive archive, and thoughtful commemorative program. Its original purpose was to record the story of those who served in the First World War, but today its mission is to assist us in remembering, interpreting, and understanding the experiences of Australians involved in wars and peacekeeping missions around the world.

The Memorial building, with its marriage of grandeur and simplicity, has become one of the nation's most recognisable – and most loved – architectural edifices.

The sandstone monolith with its Byzantine-inspired dome is remarkably at ease in its natural bush setting at the base of Mount Ainslie: kangaroos feed in the manicured grounds, and at dawn and dusk the cockatoos screech overhead before settling in nearby gum trees.

Two medieval stone lions guard the building's lobby. The lions once flanked the gateway of the Menin Road at Ypres in Belgium, through which tens of thousands of Australian soldiers passed on the way to the fighting on the Western Front. Still bearing the scars of damage from the First World War, the lions were given to the Memorial by the city of Ypres in 1936.

Past the entrance is the Commemorative Area, a sombre yet serene space and the site of the evening Last Post Ceremony. This is a quiet place to remember those who died and to reflect upon their sacrifice. It consists of a simple, symmetrical courtyard featuring the Pool of Reflection, where the Eternal Flame burns bright and constant; the cloisters, which house the Roll of Honour; and the Hall of Memory, where the Tomb of the Unknown Australian Soldier lies.

HALL OF MEMORY
HALL OF HONOUR
BOOKSHOP →
TELEPHONE →

'The Last Post Ceremony for Charlie will undoubtedly nurture our family's memory of his sacrifice long into the future. We are deeply grateful.'
Shane Negus, descendant of Private Charlie Jonas, 16th Battalion, AIF

ABOVE The Eternal Flame in the Pool of Reflection. 2017.4.125.1
RIGHT The Roll of Honour is one of the most important commemorative elements of the Memorial. PAIU2014/146.17

The classic lines and structured gardens of the courtyard are softened by water, light, and shade. Its perimeter includes 26 carved sandstone sculptures representing native birds, animals, and reptiles, as well as the faces of an Aboriginal man and woman, positioned as caretakers of the Eternal Flame and as guardians of the Tomb of the Unknown Australian Soldier.

Within the elegant cloisters are rows of bronze panels stamped with the names of the more than 102 800 Australians who have died in war or as a result of operational service. Australia is one of the few nations able to identify its war dead so completely, and the rows upon rows of names give a powerful impression of the magnitude of the loss. The Roll of Honour was not compiled in time for the Memorial's opening in 1941, but Bean regarded it as one of the most important commemorative elements:

I strongly felt that in the great hall surrounded by the ... names, Australians would feel almost the presence of the fallen – as though these themselves lay there with the great record, which they had created, lying treasured around them.[14]

Bean and Treloar worked hard to establish the parameters for inclusion on the Roll of Honour, and its content is still occasionally reviewed.

'I am a 72-year-old war veteran who is blind and I attended the Australian War Memorial with my guide dog to lay a wreath during the Last Post Ceremony for those who gave their lives serving Australia during the Malaysian Emergency and the Indonesian Confrontation – two little-known or seldom-recognised wars ... As a former soldier, being able to participate in the ceremony has left me with a profound feeling of quiet satisfaction that I was able to personally honour my mates' sacrifices, and for this I am extremely grateful. I applaud the Memorial for honouring these heroes, nightly, in such a dignified manner.'
Geoff McGibbon, veteran

Members of Australia's Federation Guard in formation around the Tomb of the Unknown Australian Soldier. 2016.8.82.2

The first challenges were determining a cut-off date for those who had died as a result of their service after the war ended, and whether the Roll should include Australians who served with allied forces.[15] In the end, the criteria for inclusion specified that individuals eligible for the Roll for pre-1914 conflicts, as well as for the First and Second World Wars, must have served as a member of the Australian armed forces, and were not included if they had served with other allied forces, or as merchant seamen. He or she must have died during active service, or as a result of that service, within specific periods (for the First World War, the start date is 4 August 1914, when the United Kingdom declared war on Germany, and the end date is 31 March 1921, when the AIF was disbanded). The criteria were widened for post-1945 conflicts to include persons who had died during or as a result of service that was also 'non-warlike', and for certain peacetime operations. Australians who died during periods of conflict but who were not serving with the Australian armed forces are on the Commemorative Roll, which was established in 1981 and is displayed in the form of a leatherbound book kept in the Commemorative Area.

Each person's name is listed on the Roll of Honour under the unit in which they served, but without military rank or honours. Bean and Treloar originally sought to have names arranged according to local town or district, but this proved difficult to research and organise. The unit listings were Bean's only concession to a military identity: he argued fervently against the inclusion of rank and decorations, telling Treloar in the 1920s that 'inclusion in the Honour Roll is given for one reason only — that these men all made the one equal sacrifice'.[16]

Installation of the Roll of Honour began in 1961, and initially included the names of servicemen and servicewomen who died in pre-1914 conflicts, the First and Second World Wars, the Korean War, and the Malayan Emergency.[17] Honour Rolls for conflicts after 1961

were added later, and new names continue to be inserted. Eligibility for the Roll of Honour is determined by the Memorial's Council, which from time to time reviews the requirements for inclusion.

The Roll of Honour has been adopted by visitors as a space for reflection and individual commemoration. In 1993, during the interment of the Unknown Australian Soldier, people waiting to lay a poppy on the tomb queued along the cloisters. By the end of the day the bronze panels were decorated with hundreds of red poppies, wedged next to the names of the fallen. This tradition has continued, and today visitors are struck by the solemn beauty of the area, lit up by thousands of bright red poppies placed by individuals who were moved by a person's service and sacrifice.

Beyond the Roll of Honour is the Hall of Memory. The circular building, with its copper-clad dome, contains one of the largest mosaics in the world, with more than six million tesserae lining its interior. Stained-glass windows on three sides of the Hall depict figures in uniforms of the First World War, and represent personal, social, and fighting qualities displayed and held dear by Australians. The windows and the mosaic were designed by Napier Waller, an artist and veteran who lost an arm at Bullecourt in May 1917.

In the centre of the Hall rests the Tomb of the Unknown Australian Soldier. Plans to honour an unknown Australian were first put forward in the 1920s, but Bean and Treloar were concerned that a tomb – then proposed for locations other than Canberra – would detract from the Memorial. Leaders of the organisation that became known as the Returned and Services League (RSL) also opposed the plan. Their allegiance was to the unknown British warrior entombed in Westminster Abbey, who at that time represented all who fought for the Empire.[18]

It was not until the early 1990s that the Memorial and the RSL relented in their opposition. And so, on Remembrance Day 1993 – the 75th anniversary of the Armistice that ended the First World War –

the Unknown Australian Soldier was entombed during an emotional ceremony attended by thousands of Australians.[19]

The remains had been recovered from a grave in Adelaide Cemetery near Villers-Bretonneux in France, where Australian soldiers had won a great victory on Anzac Day 1918. Thousands of people lined Anzac Parade for the funeral procession from Parliament House to the Memorial, where Prime Minister Paul Keating delivered a powerful eulogy, including the memorable phrase: 'He is all of them. And he is one of us.'

Millions of visitors, including heads of state from around the world, have since stood solemnly at the foot of the tomb and bowed, reflecting upon the sacrifice of those who have died in service.

Commemorative activities are an integral part of the Memorial's function. Since its opening, one of its central roles has been to organise and host the national ceremonies for Anzac Day and Remembrance Day. Over the decades, a number of other events and ceremonies have been added to the Memorial's commemorative schedule: veterans groups and school groups regularly hold wreathlaying ceremonies in the Commemorative Area or the Memorial grounds; official visitors pay tribute to Australia's war dead by laying wreaths at the Tomb of the Unknown Australian Soldier; individual unit associations dedicate plaques within the Memorial gardens; and special services are held on significant anniversaries, such as for the battle of Long Tan (1966).

'*Many elements of commemoration are drawn together in a Last Post
Ceremony: a reading, the reciting of the Ode, a piper and bugler, and the
music of 'Flowers of the Forest' and 'The Last Post'. The setting for the
ceremony – amid the Roll of Honour, Tomb of the Unknown Australian
Soldier, poppies, and rosemary – is also rich with symbolism.*'
Roslyn Elliot, Visitor Services Officer, Australian War Memorial

For decades, the memorial has ended each day with a closing ceremony. Visitors were originally invited to gather in the Commemorative Area for a brief address on the Memorial's history, followed by a recorded playing of the Last Post. Occasionally, a historian or curator would speak about a significant military action, and may have touched upon particular individuals who fought and died. In time, the Memorial employed buglers or pipers to play at the ceremony.

Today, the ceremonial closing is known as the Last Post Ceremony, which features the story of just one person listed on the Roll of Honour, and draws together current serving members, families of the fallen, school children, veterans, and the broader community. The ceremony has created a new ritual for remembrance that highlights individual service and sacrifice, and acts as a last reminder of courage and selflessness before visitors journey home.

LEFT Second World War veterans who took part in the battle of Milne Bay at the ceremony commemorating the action's 75th anniversary in 2017. 2017.4.212.30
RIGHT The Memorial is built on the same axis as Parliament House, highlighting the importance of service and remembering those lost in war. 2016.8.174.42

FAR LEFT Ben Roberts-Smith VC MG
attends the Last Post Ceremony with his
daughter on Anzac Day 2014. PA1U2014/076.05
LEFT Thousands of school children attend
Last Post Ceremonies each year. 2016.8.156.4
ABOVE Doug Baird, father of Corporal
Cameron Baird VC MG, attends the ceremony
for the 50th anniversary of the battle of
Long Tan in August 2016. 2016.8.131.25

Chaplain 3rd Class Michael Bergin MC, Australian Chaplains' Department, Australian Imperial Force

Killed in action: 12 October 1917

Born in Tipperary, Ireland, Michael Bergin was a Jesuit priest who became an admired and respected member of the Australian Imperial Force (AIF). At the outbreak of the First World War he was working at a Catholic school in Syria – then a part of the Ottoman Empire – and when Turkey entered the war on the side of Germany he was interned as an enemy civilian. After several months of imprisonment he was extradited by the Turkish government and arrived in Cairo around the same time that the first Australian troops began arriving in Egypt.

Bergin offered his services to the AIF, which was short of Roman Catholic padres, and joined the 5th Light Horse Brigade. He served on Gallipoli, but in September 1915 he was evacuated to England with serious illness. In December he was back working in various hospitals before joining the 51st Battalion. He served as chaplain in all the unit's major actions in France and Belgium, including at Pozières, Mouquet Farm, Messines, and the Third Battle of Ypres.

Defying general orders banning chaplains from entering the front lines, Bergin served alongside the men of his battalion, and was frequently found in the trenches and around the front lines, winning the admiration of all, regardless of faith. On one occasion he led a Mass in a field near Albert while under enemy artillery fire. One soldier described this scene as the most inspiring of the war.

On 12 October 1917 Bergin was killed near Zonnebeke in Belgium when a heavy shell burst near the aid post where he was working.

ABOVE Chaplain Michael Bergin defied general orders banning chaplains from entering the front lines. P09291.122
RIGHT Official war photographer Frank Hurley's iconic image of the Passchendaele campaign marks the area where Chaplain Bergin was killed in 1917. P05464.001

A photograph by Australian photographer Frank Hurley marking the area in which Bergin was killed became one of the iconic images of the Passchendaele campaign.

Bergin was buried in Reninghelst Churchyard Extension cemetery. His loss was met with great sadness throughout the 13th Brigade, and he was posthumously awarded the Military Cross. The citation praised his 'magnificent zeal and courage':

> In the line or out Padre Bergin is always to be found among his men helping them when in trouble and inspiring them with his noble example and never-failing cheerfulness. These are the characteristics which have endeared him to all and which make him such a valuable asset to the Brigade.

An Irishman by birth, Bergin was one of the very few members of the AIF never to have set foot in Australia. Regardless, he was deeply admired by the thousands of Australian soldiers with whom he served.

Dr Lachlan Grant

Ordinary Seaman Edward Sheean, HMAS *Armidale*, Royal Australian Navy

Killed in action: 1 December 1942

Born on 28 December 1923, Edward 'Teddy' Sheean was the 14th child of James and Mary Sheean. Growing up in Latrobe in northern Tasmania, he attended a local Catholic school and afterwards worked on nearby farms. Following the outbreak of war, he enlisted in the Royal Australian Navy (RAN) in April 1941. Five of his brothers also served in the forces – four in the army and one in the navy.

In June 1942 Sheean was posted to the corvette HMAS *Armidale* as an Oerlikon anti-aircraft gun-loader. The corvette was initially tasked with escort duties in the waters off northern Australia and Papua. In an undated letter to his mother, Sheean commented, 'I don't think you need to be frightened of any of us not coming back.'

The *Armidale* arrived in Darwin in early November. Later that month it and the corvette HMAS *Castlemaine* sailed to Timor to reinforce the small Australian force fighting on the island and to evacuate exhausted troops and Portuguese civilians. On 1 December the corvettes rendezvoused with the naval tender HMAS *Kuru*, which transferred its civilians to the *Castlemaine* before returning to Darwin.

The *Armidale* and *Kuru* continued towards Timor. From 12.28 pm both vessels came under repeated attack from Japanese aircraft and were separated. The *Kuru* made it back to Darwin. The *Armidale*, however, fought against attacking aircraft into the afternoon. Finally, at 3.15 pm, nine bombers, three fighters,

and a floatplane attacked the vessel. Hit by two torpedoes and possibly a bomb, it rolled over and sank in three or four minutes.

Sheean, though wounded, kept firing an Oerlikon gun even as the ship sank, and brought down a Japanese bomber. His final actions feature in many of the accounts from the *Armidale*'s survivors. Ordinary Seaman Russel Caro afterwards reported:

> Teddy died, but none of us who survived, I am sure, will ever forget his gallant deed ... When the order 'Abandon ship' was given, he made for the side, only to be hit twice by the bullets of an attacking Zero. None of us will ever know what made him do it, but he went back to his gun, strapped himself in, and brought down a Jap plane, still firing as he disappeared beneath the waves.

Only 49 of the 149 men on board the *Armidale* survived the sinking and lived to be rescued. Edward Sheean was just 18 years old.

In addition to being posthumously Mentioned in Despatches, Sheean was honoured in his hometown of Latrobe with the Teddy Sheean Memorial and the Sheean Walk. In 2001 the RAN commissioned the Collins-class submarine HMAS *Sheean*. It was the first RAN ship to be named in honour of a naval rating.

Sheean is also commemorated on the Plymouth Naval Memorial in England.

Dr Karl James

ABOVE Dale Marsh's *Ordinary Seaman Edward Sheean, HMAS* Armidale (1978) depicts Sheean firing at Japanese bombers while wounded. ART28160
LEFT Edward 'Teddy' Sheean (right) with his brother Stoker Class 2 Thomas 'Mick' Sheean. 044154

**Private George Ross Seabrook,
17th Battalion,
Australian Imperial Force**

Killed in action: 20 September 1917

**Private Theo Leslie Seabrook,
17th Battalion,
Australian Imperial Force**

Killed in action: 20 September 1917

**Second Lieutenant William
Keith Seabrook,
17th Battalion, Australian
Imperial Force**

Died of wounds: 21 September 1917

Theo (left), William 'Keith'
(centre), and George (right)
Seabrook. H05568

George (14 February 1892), Theo (17 May 1893), and William (24 March 1896) Seabrook were born to parents William and Fanny in Sydney. They grew up in the suburb of Petersham with four other siblings.

George had married Winifred Kean in 1913 and was working as a master painter when the First World War began. Theo worked at the locomotive works at Eveleigh. William, who was known by his middle name, 'Keith', had left his job as a telephonist to enlist in the Militia in August 1915, and was commissioned as lieutenant.

In mid-1916 the three Seabrook brothers enlisted in the Australian Imperial Force. By this time, George's wife had died.

Posted to the 17th Battalion, the men trained in Australia before leaving in October on the troopship *Ascanius*. They undertook further training in England, and in 1917 were sent to fight on the Western Front, first in France and then in Belgium.

Keith's previous military training stood him in good stead, but all three proved able soldiers. In July 1917 Keith was commissioned and given command of 11 Platoon in the battalion's C Company.

On 20 September 1917 the 17th Battalion attacked the German positions in front of the village of Westhoek in the battle of Menin Road. Advancing more than a kilometre, the battalion's attack was successful, but the day would prove devastating for the Seabrook family.

With a final handshake for his batman, Lieutenant Keith Seabrook was leading the men of his platoon into front-line positions when a phosphorous bomb killed or wounded the whole section.

Keith suffered severe wounds from the blast and, although he made it to a casualty clearing station, the popular young officer died the following day.

He was 21 years old.

As their younger brother was being carried from the battlefield, Privates George and Theo Seabrook were with the battalion as it launched its attack. Shortly afterwards both were hit by the same artillery shell and killed instantly. Their bodies were never found. Their names are on the Menin Gate among more than 6000 other Australians who died in Belgium with no known grave. George was 25 years old, Theo was 24.

The loss hit the family hard. Two months after the battle, their mother wrote to the military authorities seeking information about Theo and George:

It is all very confusing to our minds and if you could explain to me we would be much obliged and thankful. The blow of losing our three sons in one battle is terrible. We are heartbroken.

She later wrote to her member of parliament:

Having given our three boys as a sacrifice to the country … their loss I will never recover and now my husband is a complete wreck … I have put my property up for sale as it seems there is no other way. Mr Seabrook has been raving about our three boys and has delusions of all kinds. Please pardon me for telling you all these things, but I have no one to confide in.

Mrs Seabrook chose the epitaph for Keith's headstone in the Lijssenthoek Military Cemetery: 'A willing sacrifice for the world's peace.'

Dr Meleah Hampton

Temporary Sergeant Stafford Kenny James Lenoy, 3rd Battalion, Royal Australian Regiment, Australian Army

Killed in action: 24 April 1951

Stafford Kenny James 'Len' Lenoy was born on 21 October 1923 in Cairns, Queensland, to Octavius 'Ockie' and Janine 'Janie' Lenoy. He was the middle child in a large Indigenous Australian family.

After spending his formative years in the Queensland town of Ayr, Lenoy, his parents, and his siblings were removed by authorities and transported to Palm Island.

In March 1943, aged 18, Lenoy was called up for service in the Militia. Four days later he volunteered for service in the Second World War with the Australian Imperial Force. He did his basic and specialist training with the 2nd Australian Machine Gun Training Battalion at Tenterfield, New South Wales. He spent much of the next year in various training schools, and in May 1944 he was posted to the 2/3rd Machine Gun Battalion in the Atherton Tablelands. The battalion deployed to New Guinea in December and took part in the Aitape–Wewak campaign. After the war Lenoy transferred to the newly raised 67th Battalion at Morotai for occupation duties in Japan.

By the end of 1948 the battalion had become the 3rd Battalion, Royal Australian Regiment (3RAR). Lenoy remained with 3RAR and joined the Australian Regular Army Special Reserve in March 1950. He was soon promoted to lance corporal.

The Korean War began on 25 June 1950. Lenoy, now a member of 3RAR's medium machine-gun platoon, was deployed to Korea as part of the UN Command forces at the end of September. The battalion took part in the mobile campaign into North Korea, but in late October the UN troops were forced to withdraw as the Chinese joined the northern forces.

Following further withdrawals in January 1951, UN troops advanced again in March. Just prior to Anzac Day, 3RAR was in reserve and preparing to host their British, New Zealand, and Turkish comrades. On the morning of 23 April the Chinese launched a new offensive towards Seoul, and 3RAR, along with the 27th Brigade, was deployed north of Kapyong to stop them.

Lenoy, now a temporary sergeant, was attached to A Company in the foremost defensive positions. The Chinese forces began their attacks on the company in the late afternoon and maintained pressure throughout the night. It was during an attack in the early hours of 24 April that Stafford Lenoy was killed.

After an intense battle, the Chinese division broke off its attack on Anzac Day. For 3RAR the cost was high, with 32 men killed, 59 wounded, and three taken prisoner.

Lenoy was initially buried near Kapyong, but was later reinterred at the United Nations Memorial Cemetery at Pusan.

He was 27 years old.

Michael Kelly

Stafford 'Len' Lenoy during his service in Korea. P01813.802

Private Tom Jones, 3rd Battalion, Australian Imperial Force

Killed in action: 5 May 1917

Private Tom Jones of Condobolin,
New South Wales. P07083.001

Tom Jones was born in 1893 on Euglo Station, near Condobolin, New South Wales, to William and Louisa Jones. He was educated privately on the station and worked as a station hand before enlisting in the Australian Imperial Force at Cootamundra on 18 March 1916.

Before Jones left for active service overseas, a social evening was held in his honour at the nearby town of Bena. Despite a heavy downpour, a large group attended, and Jones was presented with a wristwatch and other gifts, while speeches were made lauding his decision to enlist. After the formalities, there was dancing until daylight.

On 26 September 1916 Private Jones left Sydney aboard the troopship *Euripides* with reinforcements to the 3rd Battalion. During the journey he was charged with disobeying orders and was given an extra day of fatigue work. This seems to have been an isolated incident, as no other disciplinary infractions were recorded before he arrived in England and joined the 1st Training Battalion.

After a period of training, Private Jones arrived in France in April 1917. At the time, many Australian battalions had been involved in the fighting around the French village of Bullecourt. Less than two weeks after joining his battalion on the Western Front, Private Jones's battalion was called into action.

In early May 1917 the 3rd Battalion was in or near the front line not far from Bullecourt. After helping to fend off a number of enemy counter-attacks on 4 May, the battalion spent the following day under a heavy German bombardment amid constant threats from long-range sniping. That evening the German troops attacked again, but their operation was broken up by the Australian artillery, which unfortunately dropped a few shells short into their own positions.

At some point in the confusion, Private Tom Jones was killed in action. No record remains of the manner of his death, and his body was not recovered from the battlefield. Today he is commemorated on the Australian National Memorial at Villers-Bretonneux, among the more than 10 000 other Australians killed in France who have no known grave.

He was 24 years old.

Dr Duncan Beard

Chapter three

The Last Post Ceremony

'Far from offering reverent portraits of idealised saints, the Last Post Ceremony presents ordinary people in extraordinary circumstances, as admirable and adventurous as anyone alive, no better than you or me, and with the same capacity for both virtue and vice. I wonder if it is even possible to remember them without understanding who they were.' Dr Duncan Beard, Editor

The names of more than 54 000 British and Commonwealth troops are listed on the Menin Gate Memorial to the Missing at Ypres in the Flanders region of Belgium. Eric Austin Tate is one of them.

Tate, a sergeant in the 20th Battalion, Australian Imperial Force (AIF), disappeared on 9 October 1917 during the battle of Poelcappelle – a turning point in the major British offensive known as the Third Battle of Ypres. The Australians had captured several kilometres of German-occupied territory in the battles of Menin Road, Polygon Wood, and Broodseinde, but at Poelcappelle the advance wallowed in mud as rain deluged the low-lying, artillery-damaged area, and adequate gun support could not be brought within range. Similarly vicious fighting in waterlogged conditions marked the battle of Passchendaele on 12 October. Australian infantry and artillery divisions sustained 38 000 casualties in the eight weeks that they were involved in the offensive, with 6673 dead in the month of October alone.

Tate's fate was the subject of an extensive search by the Red Cross Wounded and Missing Enquiry Bureau and an official army inquiry, which finally determined that he had been killed in action. In the postwar years Tate's name was added to the Menin Gate Memorial to the Missing as one of almost 6200 Australians who died in Belgium but had no known grave. It also appears as a footnote in Charles Bean's official account of the battles around Passchendaele, and is one of the more than 60 000 names inscribed on the First World War Roll of Honour at the Australian War Memorial.

FACING PAGE LEFT Eric Tate shortly after his enlistment in the Australian Imperial Force in 1915. P07715.002
FACING PAGE RIGHT Hellfire Corner along the Menin Road, the gateway to the battlefield of Ypres, 1917. E01237

'I cannot praise highly enough all of those who have a part in the organisation of the Last Post Ceremony each day. It is great that so many of those killed in action receive this type of recognition and it is wonderful for their family members to be able to participate in the ceremony.'

Ian Loiterton, descendant of Private Ronald Douglas, 17th Battalion, AIF

During his term as Australian Ambassador to Belgium, Luxembourg, the European Union, and NATO, Dr Brendan Nelson forged strong links with the communities of Flanders. As part of his public duties he made regular trips to attend Last Post Ceremonies at the Menin Gate Memorial, and he also visited in a private capacity. He was profoundly affected by the sacrifices of so many, and wondered about the personal stories of men like Tate.

Upon his appointment as Director of the Australian War Memorial, Dr Nelson saw an opportunity to strengthen the community's connection to military history through the nation's war dead. He asked historians to begin researching the names on the Roll of Honour so that an account of a person's life could be shared, and their service honoured, at the Memorial's daily closing ceremony.

'We need to remind people that every single one of those names was a person just like us, a real person who had a life, who loved and was loved, who then joined our Defence Force and gave his or her life for our nation,' he said. 'In doing so, we engage a new generation of Australians in our history.'

The primary purpose of each Last Post Ceremony is to remember and reflect upon the loss of an individual who died as a result of their war or operational service. Its broader aims are to help people understand the experience of war and its enduring impact on society, and to inform the public about the many conflicts and peacekeeping operations in which the nation has been involved.

Families of servicemen and servicewomen who have died, veterans, and the broader community have reported overwhelmingly positive appreciation of the project. It has also benefited military scholarship by giving historians an opportunity to dispel long-held myths about the Anzacs, including with regard to the racial and cultural composition of our armed forces. In particular, the contribution of Indigenous Australians to our military history has been more closely examined and uncovered. The project has highlighted lesser-known theatres of war, drawing national attention to campaigns that may have been previously overlooked or overshadowed by the more commonly told stories of Gallipoli and Kokoda. The Last Post stories also expose the realities of soldiering: while there is honour in the service and sacrifice of each person listed on the Roll, they did not all die gloriously.

Sickness and disease, as well as accidents, are regularly listed as causes of death. The conditions that servicemen and servicewomen endure can likewise cause physical and emotional stress, loneliness, and boredom, which may lead to rule-breaking – or to breakdowns. Ultimately, those who have served and died in war represent a cross-section of society, which can expose uncomfortable truths: as in any large population, criminals and abusers are among the thousands of those who have served and died.

Anger, despair, mishap, hate, betrayal, and complacency are all found in the stories of the dead listed on the Roll. Just as common are acts of courage, grace, kindness, goodwill, selflessness, and love. The bravery and stoicism of men and women in trying conditions and dangerous circumstances are recurring themes: from the pilot shot down during a bombing raid on Germany to the nurse who died in Japanese captivity.

The vast majority of Australia's serving men and women have not been formally researched, and investigating each individual on the Roll of Honour usually takes hours of painstaking inquiry. The biographies are crafted from source material held in public archives, libraries, and cultural institutions. Historians generally start their investigations with an

'The Last Post Ceremony project is producing what I believe is already, and what will likely continue to become, a world-class historical resource. Students and researchers will one day have access to detailed and extensive histories of not only key battles and units but also every single Australian soldier who gave their life in service of their country. This is unprecedented in world historiography. I am proud to work on the Last Post Ceremonies not only as a way to honour the sacrifice of so many but also to provide a meaningful and lasting contribution to Australian history.'

David Sutton, Historian

individual's service record, before examining unit war diaries, embarkation records and nominal rolls, accounts in official histories, newspapers, other publications, casualty reports and flight log books, war graves records, and Red Cross files. Information from families about siblings, nicknames, and character traits needs to be verified. A search of the Memorial's collection may also uncover personal diaries and letters, photographs, medals, and other items that reveal more about the person and their military service. Each completed story is thoroughly checked by the Memorial's editors.

It can be difficult, however, to find details of people who died in war: some went missing without a trace, while others left little public mark – their lives before the war were lived quietly, without mentions in official records, or quickly, going off to war as young adults yet to fulfil their dreams. There is poignancy in the scant detail as well as the particulars.

Sergeant Eric Tate's story was told at a Last Post Ceremony on 5 September 2014. Like many other First World War infantrymen, his experience was a mix of anticipation, optimism, frustration, disenchantment, and tragedy. He was born in 1892 to Emma and George Tate in the small hamlet of Kangaroo Valley in New South Wales. George bred champion dairy cattle on his property, 'Oakdale', and was prominent in the community.[20] Eric was a talented athlete and footballer, well known in the surrounding districts for his sporting prowess.[21] He also developed a keen interest in pedigree stock and, after his father's death in 1911, Eric and his siblings managed the family farm.

Tate was 23, and had a girlfriend named Flo,[22] when he enlisted in the AIF in late October 1915. He was posted to the 20th Battalion and embarked for overseas service within a few days of joining up, leaving Sydney on 2 November. During the early stages of the voyage he wrote to his mother: 'I am going away feeling well and I always feel that I'm going to see things through and get back again.'[23]

'The ceremony was a fitting tribute and sober reminder of my grandfather's short life. He was a man who has endured for us through stories and memories and these are all we have, but for a brief moment he was brought to life for us all. For my father this was a day of reflection mixed with nervous anticipation. He told me that this day was by far up the list of his life experiences, and he included his wedding day and the birth of his children in that list.'
Libby Heasman, granddaughter of Acting Corporal Donald Atkinson, 2/18th Battalion, Second AIF

RIGHT Wounded men on the Menin Road during the battle on 20 September 1917. E00711

Tate contracted mumps en route to Egypt, and had a brief stint in hospital upon arrival before moving to a training camp on the outskirts of Cairo. He spent the next few months on long marches, in rifle drills, and practicing mock attacks in the desert.

The 20th Battalion shipped to France in March 1916, and entered the trenches of the Western Front in April. Tate wrote to his mother on 9 May that the 'very quiet spot' of the line they were holding had for a few hours suddenly become 'simply hell let loose', adding, 'The Gallipoli boys all admit that they never went through anything nearly so severe while they were on the Pen[insula].'[24]

The unit took part in its first major action around Pozières between late July and the end of August 1916. Tate's emerging leadership skills saw him promoted to lance corporal, but that autumn he contracted tonsillitis. After several weeks in hospital he returned to his battalion as the wet and miserable winter of 1916 set in. It wasn't long before the harsh conditions saw him develop a severe case of trench foot. He was sent to England in late December for treatment and convalescence.

By now Tate had lost his enthusiasm for the war. He longed to stay in England, and hinted in a letter to his brother George that he would probably break the rules and take a few extra days off when he was granted leave. 'I reckon if the mothers of Britain could see the battlefield of the Somme they'd rebel,' he wrote on 30 January 1917.[25] When he did return to his unit in France in early May 1917, it was to learn that his best mate had been killed just hours before.[26]

At one point Tate had claimed that he didn't really care for promotions, because they seemed to put him in more danger, but by August he had risen to the rank of sergeant.[27] He took part in the fierce fighting of the battle of Menin Road in September and, two weeks later, was at the attack at Poelcappelle. Tate went missing during the battle and it was later determined that he had been hit by a shell on the first day, and died instantly.[28]

A few weeks after Tate went missing, Sergeant Herbert Inman, also of the 20th Battalion, wrote to Tate's mother:

I have been a close friend of his ever since he joined us on the Desert and have never had a better mate. He was liked by all his fellow Sergeants and in fact by everyone he came in contact with. As a soldier he had the confidence of all the Officers, NCOs and men, and always done his duty, to the smallest detail ...

This War has claimed some fine men, but not one better than your son, and his death has cast a gloom over all of us who are left.[29]

Sergeant Eric Tate was 26 years old.

LEFT A mule team bogged in the deep mud around Ypres during the Passchendaele campaign, October 1917. E00962

Every Last Post Ceremony held at the Australian War Memorial involves the work of a team of dedicated staff: curators, photographers, editors, event planners, communications specialists, IT and audio visual technicians, visitor service providers, and educators.

At 4.55 pm each day the ceremony begins with the singing of the National Anthem, followed by the strains of a lament, played by a piper. As music fills the Commemorative Area, visitors are invited to lay wreaths and floral tributes beside the Pool of Reflection. A uniformed member of the Australian Defence Force (ADF) reads an account of the life and military service of a person listed on the Roll of Honour, followed by the recitation of the Ode (see page 96). A bugler plays the Last Post, and the ceremony concludes as the doors to the Hall of Memory are closed.

'The biography, the bagpiper and bugler, the wreathlaying, the framed photo of my uncle – all left me overwhelmed and quite emotional. My heartfelt thanks to all who assisted at the ceremony.'
Brigid Healy, niece of Lance Corporal George Stolz, No. 1 Australian Stationary Hospital, AIF

LEFT A large crowd gathered for the Last Post Ceremony on the 100th anniversary of the battle of Pozières, July 2016. 2016.8.110.26
RIGHT Staff member Gary Wheatley with floral tributes before a ceremony. 2016.8.104.1

'It's a wonderful way to finish our business day here at the Memorial, and an opportunity to quietly reflect and remember those who gave the ultimate sacrifice – and why we actually work here.'
Richard Cruise, Manager of Visitor Services

Each story starts with a name. An individual may be chosen because of their connection to a significant action, unit, or group, particularly when it coincides with an anniversary – such as Sergeant Richard Leslie Spunner, who was honoured on the 75th anniversary of the sinking of the Japanese prisoner transport ship *Montevideo Maru*. Families can also request a Last Post Ceremony as a tribute to a loved one or ancestor, and historians may choose their subject according to a particular research interest.

While the stories are being written, the Last Post team schedules the event and communicates with families who have made requests, coordinates ADF personnel, and organises the attendance of dignitaries and special groups at a ceremony.

The Visitor Services team manages the daily delivery of the event, organising Master of Ceremonies functions, ensuring wreaths are in place for presentation, assisting visitors, families, and school groups, and advising the Defence reader on their duties.

LEFT Staff member Philip Sneeuwjagt instructs visiting school students on proceedings before a ceremony. 2017.4.240.1
ABOVE Staff member Richard Cruise regularly acts as the Memorial's Master of Ceremonies. 2016.8.230.23

'When my father died on a bamboo bed ... at the 55 Kilo Camp on 20 September 1943, I can only imagine what his last thoughts would have been. However, I am certain that he would not have had the slightest thought that nearly 71 years to the day, three generations born to him would be at the Australian War Memorial remembering and honouring him, with many other friends watching the live broadcast across Australia and also as far as the United Kingdom.'

Jim Busine, son of Private Sydney Busine, 2/30th Battalion, Second AIF

More than 135 000 students visit the Memorial every year, and teachers regularly request that excursions include the late afternoon event. The Memorial's education experts manage their attendance.

Photographers are often called upon to capture the occasion, particularly when it is attended by international dignitaries or other prominent figures. The Memorial's multimedia team reproduces a photograph of the deceased, where available, to be displayed by the Pool of Reflection.

A live broadcast of the ceremony is streamed daily on the Memorial's website.

This initiative is supported by the RSL & Services Clubs Association, RSL Victoria, and RSL Queensland, and makes the event accessible to all Australians and to communities overseas. The ceremonies are also recorded and visitors can buy a copy as a permanent memento of the occasion.

Commemoration through understanding is at the heart of the memorial. That is why it is dedicated to honouring, through the Last Post Ceremony, all 102 800 servicemen and servicewomen listed on the Roll of Honour, ensuring their lives are part of our national story – lest we forget.

LEFT A visitor captures scenes of a ceremony. 2017.4.65.7
RIGHT Two young visitors watch the ceremony from the cloisters. PA1U2015/179.26
FOLLOWING PAGES Visitors take a moment for reflection after a ceremony. 2017.4.168.16

'Witnessing the positive and moving effect the Last Post Ceremony has on our visitors is incredibly rewarding. Every evening, the story of the life and death of a single serviceman or servicewoman reminds us of the important and privileged role we have in ensuring a nation remembers.'

Sarah Hitchcock, Head of Commemoration and Visitor Engagement

The Ode

They shall grow not old, as we that are left grow old;

Age shall not weary them, nor the years condemn.

At the going down of the sun and in the morning

We will remember them.

'The Ode' is taken from the fourth stanza of the poem 'For the Fallen' by Laurence Binyon (1869–1943). The poem was first published in *The London Times* in 1914, and in following years was a popular inclusion in anthologies of war verse. It was selected to accompany the unveiling of the London Cenotaph in 1919 and, like so many commemorative traditions, was adopted across the Commonwealth. Binyon's poem was also read at the laying of the Inauguration Stone at the Australian War Memorial in 1929.[30]

RIGHT Warrant Officer Joanne Davy salutes after reciting the Ode. 2016.8.110.71

LEFT Cadets line the Pool of Reflection at a Last Post Ceremony. 2016.8.110

RIGHT Staff member Roslyn Elliot with members of the United States Air Force Academy during a wreathlaying in 2017. 2017.4.69.3

FOLLOWING PAGES LEFT School students lay wreaths at a ceremony in 2015. PAIU2015/054.17

FOLLOWING PAGES RIGHT Australia's Federation Guard conducts a catafalque party twice a month, and at ceremonies for special occasions. 2016.8.140.4

ABOVE Visitors to the ceremony with
Director Dr Brendan Nelson. 2017.4.126.37
RIGHT The Last Post Ceremony takes place
each evening, rain or shine. 2017.4.172.23

Lance Corporal John Hill,
2/4th Machine Gun Battalion,
Second Australian Imperial Force

Died of disease: 11 March 1943

Lance Corporal John Hill, who
died a prisoner of war in Changi,
Singapore, in 1943. P01814.001

Lance Corporal John Hill was one of thousands of Indigenous Australians to serve during the Second World War. He was born on 1 January 1912 in Fremantle, Western Australia, to Arthur and Margaret Hill. A member of the Wardandi Nation, John was the eldest of nine children. He grew up in a weatherboard cottage named 'Snake Gully' in the small seaside town of Busselton.

In the years before the Second World War, John and his brother Roy found work contracting and wheat-carting in the wheat belt area of rural Western Australia. On 23 October 1940, John enlisted in the Second Australian Imperial Force (AIF), Roy enlisted in the Royal Australian Air Force, and another brother, Harold, enlisted in the Royal Australian Navy.

John was posted to the 2/4th Machine Gun Battalion, a support unit for the 8th Division, and qualified as a mechanic and transport driver. He was promoted to lance corporal and assigned as a driver of a Bren gun carrier.

Following Japan's entry into the war in December 1941, the 2/4th Machine Gun Battalion was sent to join units of the 8th Division in Malaya. However, Japanese attacks on New Britain forced the convoy, then based in Darwin, to travel the long way around Australia, via Sydney and Fremantle. It did not reach Singapore until the end of January.

By then the Japanese had captured Malaya and were preparing to invade Singapore. As the fighting increased during the battle of Singapore, Lance Corporal Hill was wounded in the arm and head. Despite this, he still managed to drive his Bren gun carrier, with its dead and wounded crew members, back to an aid post.

Singapore fell to the Japanese on 15 February 1942 and Hill became one of 45 000 Australian and British troops captured in the surrender. He was sent to Selarang Barracks in the large prisoner-of-war camp at Changi, and later to the camp at Adam Park, where he was employed on work parties around Singapore.

In late February 1943 Hill contracted dysentery. He was sent to the hospital in Changi but died from his illness on 11 March, aged 31. He was buried the following day in the camp's AIF Cemetery in Changi.

Harold and Roy Hill both survived the war. Harold had joined the crew of HMAS *Perth*, and when that vessel was sunk he, too, became a prisoner of the Japanese. He was put to work on the Burma–Thailand Railway, and later wrote a memoir of his experiences.

Roy Hill became a pilot and an officer in Bomber Command. Serving in Britain, he flew Lancaster bombers for No. 106 and No. 189 Squadrons of the Royal Air Force.

Following the war's end John Hill's remains were reinterred in the British and Commonwealth war cemetery at Kranji, Singapore. The cross that marked his grave in Changi was collected by his mates and brought back to Australia. It was later donated to the Australian War Memorial.

The epitaph chosen by his family for his grave in Singapore bears the inscription: 'His duty nobly done. Ever remembered'.

Dr Lachlan Grant

Lieutenant Gordon Vincent Oxenham, No. 1 Squadron, Australian Flying Corps, Australian Imperial Force

Killed in action: 27 June 1918

Gordon Vincent Oxenham was born in Sydney in 1893, one of nine children born to Humphrey and Elizabeth Oxenham. The Oxenhams were a notable family: Humphrey was well-known in Australian horse-racing circles, particularly after one of his horses, Sheet Anchor, won the 1885 Melbourne Cup; while the eldest son represented New South Wales and Australia in Rugby Union. Gordon attended St Ignatius' College at Riverview, and was working as a grazier when he enlisted in the Australian Imperial Force in February 1916.

Gordon Oxenham was initially assigned to the 53rd Battalion, but was soon transferred to an officers' training school. He was appointed second lieutenant in the Australian Flying Corps and left Australia on HMAT *Suevic* in June 1917. He arrived in England a few months later but was sent on to Egypt in early 1918. There he received his 'wings', and was taken on strength with No. 1 Squadron of the Australian Flying Corps.

On 27 June 1918 Oxenham and his observer, Lieutenant Laurence Smith, were escorting a reconnaissance plane over Palestine when they were engaged by German aircraft. The reconnaissance plane successfully took down its attackers and Oxenham dived on another enemy plane several times in an attempt to destroy it, but came under fire from the ground. According to Smith, Oxenham was shot through the head and died instantly. The plane hit the ground and was badly damaged. Smith survived the crash, was taken prisoner, and spent the rest of the war in Ottoman captivity.

Though Smith reported that Oxenham was buried by the enemy, the grave could not be located after the war. Instead, Lieutenant Oxenham is commemorated on the Jerusalem Memorial in the city's war cemetery, which lists some 3300 British and dominion servicemen who died in Egypt and Palestine during the First World War but have no known grave.

Gordon Oxenham was 24.

Dr Kate Ariotti

RIGHT Australian Flying Corps trainees and instructors with a Curtiss Jenny aircraft in 1917. Lieutenant Oxenham is second from right in the front row. P00731.005

Sister Caroline Mary Ennis,
10th Australian General Hospital,
Australian Army Nursing Service,
Second Australian Imperial Force

Drowned: 14 February 1942

Sister Caroline Ennis was one of
65 Australian nurses on board the
ship *Vyner Brooke* when it was
bombed by Japanese aircraft in
February 1942. P02783.015

Caroline Ennis was born in Swan Hill on 13 August 1913 to Hugh Martin Ennis and Mary Josephine Graham of Moyhu, Victoria. She trained to be a nurse at Beechworth Hospital and passed her final examinations in March 1936.

Ennis was living in Cheshunt, Victoria, when she enlisted in the Second Australian Imperial Force in August 1940 as part of the Australian Army Nursing Service. She was attached to the 10th Australian General Hospital (AGH) and, in February 1941, embarked for service in Singapore.

Sent with her unit to Malaya, Ennis was variously detached for duty between the 10th AGH, the 2/9th Field Ambulance, and the 2/4th Casualty Clearing Station, treating the ill and wounded across the peninsula.

Ennis was working at the 2/4th Casualty Clearing Station when the Japanese invaded Malaya on 8 December 1941 – the same day as the attack on Pearl Harbor. As the enemy forces advanced along the peninsula, the nurses were made to withdraw to Singapore and rejoin the 13th AGH, the only Australian hospital left in Malaya.

Once the fall of Singapore became inevitable, most Australian civilian and nursing personnel were evacuated from the island, but nurses of the 13th AGH remained until 12 February – three days before the British forces surrendered to the Japanese. Sister Caroline Ennis was one of 65 Australian nurses who left Singapore aboard the *Vyner Brooke*, which was also carrying civilians.

Two days later the ship was bombed by the Japanese. As the bombs exploded, the nurses prepared for evacuation, rushing to treat the wounded as best they could before abandoning ship with the rest. Some were helped into lifeboats, others clung to rafts. Those who could swim made for nearby Banka Island.

Sister Ennis and Sister Betty Jeffrey each grabbed a child and ran for the ship's bridge, only to find it ablaze. After helping other passengers, they eventually managed to climb onto a raft with five other nurses on it. The raft drifted away from the wreckage, caught in the strong currents, passing other survivors during the night. Ennis had taken responsibility for the children and held them as they slept. On the second day, two of the nurses, Jeffrey and Iole Harper, volunteered to lighten the vessel and instead swam for the land. The raft, however, could not beat the current and continued to drift further out to open sea. Ennis was last seen cradling two small children – a Chinese boy and an English girl – as the raft disappeared. It was never seen again.

Caroline Ennis was 28 years old.

Christina Zissis

Private Dal Edward Abbott, 1st Battalion, Royal Australian Regiment, Australian Army

Killed in action: 30 May 1968

Originally from Ashfield in New South Wales, Dal Abbott was conscripted under the National Service Scheme in March 1967. He underwent basic training in New South Wales at Kapooka before being posted to Singleton for infantry training. In September 1967 he was posted to the 1st Battalion, Royal Australian Regiment (1RAR), where he became a member of 3 Section in 7 Platoon, C Company.

Abbott enjoyed the battalion's intense training in preparation for deployment to South Vietnam, and he was proud of his mates and the unit in which they served. He was known as a quiet but friendly young man, someone who fitted in easily with the wider unit, and was held in high regard by his fellow soldiers, officers, and NCOs. In the weeks leading up to deployment, Abbott spent as many of his weekend leaves as he could with his much-loved parents and fiancée.

Abbott's battalion deployed for its tour in Vietnam, relieving 7RAR on 9 April 1968. Soldiers were involved in patrols, reconnaissance, searches, and security operations. In May 1RAR was sent north of Saigon for Operation Toan Thang, which aimed to block the retreat of communist forces following the second communist offensive. On 12 May 1RAR set up Fire Support Base (FSB) Coral, which twice held up under heavy attack in the ensuing days.

On the morning of 30 May, C Company conducted an attack to discover the position and strength of the enemy.

Just before 9 am, the Australians were engaged by the Viet Cong and, while in pursuit, came up against a bunker system containing at least a company of North Vietnamese Army (NVA) regulars. The NVA, using small arms, machine-guns, and rockets, opened fire and engaged the rear elements of C Company with mortar fire. The officer commanding C Company immediately requested reinforcements and artillery strikes.

Dal Abbott was the number 2 on his section's machine-gun, his job being to provide protection to the gunner, load new ammunition belts into the gun and assist with any stoppages to the gun. As gunner Private Bob McLean began to fire the second belt, the weapon had a stoppage. McLean struggled to clear the gun and Abbott moved to assist his mate. When Abbott raised his head to assess the problem, he was shot and killed instantly.

With the NVA threatening to outflank the forward platoons, the Australians were forced to retire, and Abbott's body was left behind. Fire support arrived shortly after in the form of Centurion tanks sent from FSB Coral, turning the battle in favour of the Australians. Dal Abbott's body was recovered and his remains were sent with the agreement of his family to Malaysia, where he was laid to rest in the Terendak Military Cemetery.

Dal Abbott was 21 years old.

Michael Kelly

ROYAL AUSTRALIAN
INFANTRY CORPS
ROYAL AUSTRALIAN REGIMENT
I BATTALION

ABBOTT D. E.	COX R. J.
ANNESLEY F. J.	COXON R. E.
BAILEY E. J.	DAWSON I. K.
BAXTER L. J.	DONNELLY W.
BOURKE M. A.	EVANS P.
CARROLL W. T.	FIELD R. E.
CLARK C.	FOTHERINGHAM

Chapter four

The families of the fallen

RIGHT The family of Trooper David 'Poppy' Pearce, who was killed in Afghanistan in 2007, at a Last Post Ceremony in his honour in 2014.
PAIU2014/148.30

War has touched many Australian families over the last century: in service, on the home front, or in its wake. Among the most affected are those whose loved ones went to war and did not return. Their loss and sadness can endure for generations, and this grief has fostered a community that is committed to commemoration.

Official days of public remembrance are traditionally inclusive in their tributes to the fallen. Consequently, most people whose names are on the Roll of Honour are known only to their families and friends – or else have been forgotten over time. In this sense, Last Post Ceremonies give the families of the war dead a public occasion at which to remember the life and service of their loved one. Each event also acknowledges those left behind, which can give comfort to the bereaved.

The Memorial's Last Post Ceremony was introduced as Australia prepared to commemorate the centenary of the First World War, and many of the family requests that followed were from descendants of the men and women whose lives were claimed in that conflict. But the inaugural Last Post Ceremony honoured a serviceman killed in the war in Afghanistan, at the time an ongoing military commitment for Australia. Private Robert Poate's name was one of the most

recent to be added to the Roll of Honour, and for his family and the families of others killed in that conflict the loss was still raw. Robert's father Hugh Poate later reflected:

> It was a great honour for us that Robert's story was chosen to begin the daily Last Post Ceremonies. I think Robert epitomised most of the 102 800 names on the Roll of Honour in that he was only 23 years old – about the same age as most of those killed in action – he was brave, an exceptionally good soldier, well known and liked by his fellow colleagues, and a bit of a larrikin.[31]

On average, three Last Post Ceremonies per week are arranged in response to family requests, and these have proved so important to families that the waiting list currently stretches beyond two years. Relatives will often travel across Australia, or from abroad, to attend the ceremony, which can be an opportunity for family reunions. Occasionally, this happens by coincidence, like at the Last Post Ceremony for Private Alexander Stanley Clingan, who was killed at the battle of Fromelles on 19 July 1916. Descendant Chris Wright wrote afterwards that some members of the Clingan family from

Victoria had been on a trip around Australia when they arrived in Canberra without any prior knowledge that their ancestor was being commemorated:

> On the day [of] the Last Post Ceremony we met new relatives and laid a wreath beside theirs to honour and remember Alexander. [It] brought together branches of the family of a young man killed 97 years [earlier].[32]

On 2 January 2017, Joan Quinlan and 40 other family members attended the ceremony commemorating her uncle, First World War Private William Daly, who had lied about his age to enlist in the Australian Imperial Force at just 17. On 28 February 1917 his unit was heavily shelled in reserve trenches near the village of Le Barque. Daly's legs were severed below the knees by shrapnel, and he died of wounds soon after, days short of his 18th birthday. In a letter of thanks after the ceremony, his niece wrote:

> Of course, none of us knew our uncle, but since that evening we have shared our memories and we have found a common thread – somehow it has given us all a sense of closure. Although I have had the privilege of visiting my uncle's grave in faraway France, the Last Post Ceremony gave me something else which is difficult to define ... Will's family never had the opportunity to celebrate his life in such a way – surely something that would have given them great comfort.[33]

'The ceremony was so respectfully done and [the biography] so accurately researched and written, that I, and all our family members, were deeply touched.'
Bernie Mackson, great nephew of Lance Corporal
Thomas Walsh, 55th Battalion, AIF

LEFT The family of Warrant Officer Gordon Duff following a Last Post Ceremony in his honour, 24 October 2017. 2017.4.273.4

RIGHT The ceremony on 25 August 2017, commemorating the 75th anniversary of the start of the battle of Milne Bay, was attended by a number of veterans and families who lost loved ones in the Second World War action. 2017.4.212.42

The chance to learn about an ancestor's life, or to solve a mystery about their death, is a starting point for many who request Last Post Ceremonies. Stories about a family member's service are often passed down through generations, but over time various myths, inconsistencies, and vagaries can creep in. Research by the Memorial's historians can resolve questions about a person's length of service, where they fought, and how they died. In some cases, families have discovered more ancestors on the Roll of Honour. Vietnam veteran Vin Cosgrove began looking into his family tree after two of his wife's uncles were commemorated in Last Post Ceremonies:

> We had never been told by our mother and father that
> they both had uncles killed in the First World War.
> My grandmother, whose brothers were killed, was at my
> going away party, and my coming home party – nothing was
> ever mentioned about the uncles ... It turns out we have five
> great-uncles buried on the Western Front. It opened up
> a completely new chapter of history in our family.[34]

Ceremonies can be intensely personal experiences. Having attended the ceremony for Second World War Flight Sergeant Lance Anthony Stegman, his sister later relayed that it had given her a chance 'to finally say goodbye'[35] to her brother, almost 70 years after he was shot down over Germany while serving with No. 163 Squadron, Royal Air Force. Other relations had travelled from Sydney, Brisbane, and the United States to honour Stegman, who was 21 years old when he was killed. Family member Group Captain James Dickson RAAF (Retd) wrote:

> The [ceremony] highlighted that it is not only the sacrifice of
> the serviceman or servicewoman that should be recognised,
> but that the never-ending sadness and sacrifice of the family
> should also be acknowledged and not forgotten.[36]

'Thank you for staging the Last Post service for [AHS] Centaur victims, and for the reading of the life story of my mother's cousin, Private Jack Lynagh. The service meant a lot to us and has crafted strong memories that will last the rest of our lifetimes.'
Ross Peake, cousin to Private Jack Lynagh

RIGHT Nancy and Vin Cosgrove
at the Last Post Ceremony on
Vietnam Veterans Day in 2017.
2017.4.205.38

'It was special to lay the wreaths. It was a bit sad to think about the soldiers.'

Leo Cosgrove (aged 8), grandson of Vin and Nancy Cosgrove

'We get to meet so many people from across the country and they all have a different story to share with us about their loved one. It's lovely to get nice feedback from those families we've delivered a story for, but really it's an absolute honour to be able to meet them, listen to them and assist them with the ceremony.'
Jennifer Surtees,
Last Post Ceremony team

This unceasing grief was likewise carried by Roma Page for decades. Her husband, Captain Robert 'Bob' Charles Page, was a secret operative with Z Special Unit during the Second World War. He and Roma married on 1 November 1943 upon his return from Operation Jaywick, in which a crew of 14 used the dilapidated Japanese-built fishing vessel MV *Krait* to sneak into enemy waters and blow up enemy ships.

In September 1944, during Operation Rimau, Page was captured by the Japanese. He was executed on 7 July 1945 – one month before the war's end.

Page's Last Post Ceremony was held on 1 November 2013, which would have been his and Roma's 70th wedding anniversary. Roma had never remarried, and the wreath she placed by the Pool of Reflection included flowers saved from their wedding cake.

LEFT Roma Page with a portrait of her husband, Bob Page. PAIU2013/211.18
RIGHT The wreath placed by Roma Page by the Pool of Reflection included flowers saved from her wedding cake. PAIU2013/211.06

Despite the sombre nature of the ceremonies, Memorial staff receive many letters and expressions of thanks from grateful families, while participating members of the Australian Defence Force also report positive responses from attending relatives. The descendants of Sergeant Henry Alexander Black were so appreciative of the opportunity to commemorate his life and service that his 90-year-old niece, Moyah Keady (née Black), made a significant donation to the Memorial to assist with research into the roles played by Australian soldiers 'like Henry'[37] in the First World War. Cecilia Hannon sent a batch of homemade Anzac biscuits to the Memorial to thank staff for organising and hosting the ceremony remembering her great uncle Private John Tucker, who was killed in action in France on 17 August 1918. Phil Taylor, whose grandfather Able Seaman Charles William was killed in the sinking of HMAS *Parramatta* on 27 November 1941, later wrote a letter of gratitude echoing the feelings of many families who become involved in the Last Post Ceremonies:

There are no words of thanks that would be enough to adequately describe our experiences at the War Memorial. For my elderly mother in particular, this day was the closing of a chapter in her life which has taken 75 years to heal. [It] allowed her to grieve and feel the appreciation from our nation for her loss and her father's sacrifice.[38]

The Last Post Ceremony has given countless visitors the opportunity to honour a family member who died as a result of war or operational service. In this way, individual Australians whose names are listed on the Roll of Honour have had a brief light shone on their lives and their contribution to the nation.

LEFT The chance to learn about an ancestor's life, or to solve a mystery about their death, is a starting point for many who request a Last Post Ceremony. 2017.4.217.10

ABOVE LEFT Descendants of Trooper Walter Edward Smale, 2nd Australian Light Horse Regiment, pay tribute to the First World War soldier at the Last Post Ceremony on 8 August 2017. 2017.4.197.9

ABOVE RIGHT Madeline Kingsford lays a wreath in honour of her father at a ceremony requested by Legacy, a charity that helps Australian families who have lost loved ones who served, December 2016. 2016.8.236.5

Lieutenant Colonel Edgar Leslie Cecil Willis Walker Maygar VC DSO, 8th Light Horse Regiment, Australian Imperial Force

Died of wounds: 1 November 1917

E dgar Maygar was born on 27 May 1868 at Dean Station near Kilmore, Victoria. Known as 'Leslie', he was educated at Kilmore and Alexandra state schools, and afterwards became a partner on the family property at Strathearn Estate in Euroa.

Keenly interested in horses and cavalry, Maygar joined the Victorian Mounted Rifles in March 1891. He tried to enlist for active service in South Africa, but was initially kept at home by a decayed tooth.

Maygar was eventually accepted into the 5th Contingent, arriving in South Africa with his unit in February 1901. After joining a British column operating in Eastern Transvaal, he participated in various actions throughout May and June, and in August transferred with the regiment to Nataal to assist in operations against Boer commandos. During an engagement at Geelhoutboom on 23 November, Maygar saw a group of men at risk of being outflanked and rode out to order them to retire. When one of the men's horses was shot from beneath him, Maygar gave him his own horse so he could gallop for cover while Maygar made his way back on foot. For his actions that day Maygar was awarded the Victoria Cross.

Back in Australia Maygar carried his commission into the 8th Light Horse Regiment and made captain in the 16th (Indi)

Light Horse Regiment in July 1912. He enlisted in the Australian Imperial Force as soon as the First World War broke out in 1914, lowering his age by four years. He formed part of the advance party that established the light horse camp at Broadmeadows, and was made captain and posted as the commanding officer of B Squadron, 4th Light Horse Regiment. Sailing for Egypt in October 1914, Maygar took part in the fighting on Gallipoli the following year and, in October, was promoted to temporary lieutenant colonel and given command of the 8th Light Horse Regiment.

Maygar was in command of the last party to withdraw from the trenches at Anzac Cove and deemed the evacuation 'a marvellous piece of military strategy probably never equalled in all the annals of history'.

Maygar continued to command the 8th Light Horse Regiment in its campaign against the Ottoman Turks in Sinai and Palestine. He was awarded the Distinguished Service Order in June 1917 for his leadership during attacks at Magdhaba and Rafa, and was twice Mentioned in Despatches.

On 31 October 1917 Australian Light Horse units took part in the famous charge on Ottoman positions at Beersheba, Palestine. That evening Maygar received orders to retire his men to divisional headquarters. He had just returned to his column to do so when a German aircraft strafed them with machine-guns and bombs. Maygar was hit; his arm was shattered and his horse bolted, carrying him into the darkness. He was later found, but had lost so much blood that he died in hospital the following morning. He was buried in the Beersheba War Cemetery.

Maygar was revered by his men as a popular and capable commander. According to official historian Henry Gullett: 'He had in every crisis stirred the spirit of his regiment by his example in the firing line. He was a true fighting commander.'

Edgar Maygar was 42 years old.

Dr Aaron Pegram

LEFT Edgar 'Leslie' Maygar was awarded a Victoria Cross for his actions in the Boer War. P01285.001
RIGHT The medal group of Lieutenant Colonel Edgar Maygar. REL03067

Flight Lieutenant Lynne Elizabeth Rowbottom, Health Services Flight Townsville, Royal Australian Air Force

Helicopter crash: 2 April 2005

Lynne Rowbottom was born in 1962, the youngest child of Les and Pat Eadie of the Launceston suburb of Mowbray, Tasmania. She attended Invermay Primary School, and then Broadland House Girls Grammar School. She undertook nursing training at Launceston General Hospital and Queen Victoria Hospital. After working in intensive care and the renal unit, in 1991 she moved to Townsville General Hospital in Queensland and specialised in renal therapy.

She was married to Terry Rowbottom, and had one son, Rhys.

Rowbottom joined the Royal Australian Air Force (RAAF) as a nursing officer in 1996, aged 34. She had various postings during her career, was promoted to flight lieutenant in 1999, and by 2001 was back in Townsville with Health Services Flight. In 2003 she served with the Australian peacekeeping force in East Timor as part of Operation Citadel. Rowbottom was described as a proud and devoted nurse who loved her work.

In 2005 Rowbottom was attached to HMAS *Kanimbla* as it participated in Operation Sumatra Assist, Australia's contribution to disaster relief following the 2004 Boxing Day tsunami.

On 28 March 2005 *Kanimbla* was docked in Singapore when an earthquake struck off the west coast of northern Sumatra. There was widespread destruction of buildings, roads, bridges, and vital infrastructure on the island of Nias. Official reports listed 850 people killed and more than 6000 injured. HMAS *Kanimbla* was immediately deployed to the island to provide medical and transport support to Indonesian authorities in what became known as Operation Sumatra Assist II.

With the roads damaged, medical support could not reach remote areas, so *Kanimbla* deployed one of its Sea King helicopters to deliver medical teams and humanitarian supplies to the island.

On the afternoon of 2 April, RAAF helicopter *Shark 02* flew towards Nias with its regular crew of four, along with seven medical and communications specialists from the navy and air force. Reaching the village of Tuindrao on the island's west coast, the helicopter prepared to land on the local football pitch. As it approached its landing, it suddenly pitched forward and struck the ground. A crew member later recalled, 'One minute the ground seemed a fair way below us, and the next it was close and coming through the cockpit'. The helicopter flipped onto its back, fell to its side, and burst into flames. Locals managed to pull two badly injured personnel from the flaming wreckage, but nine others were killed, including Flight Lieutenant Rowbottom.

The remains of the deceased were transported to Australia three days later, and their families were joined at a ceremony by the Governor-General of Australia, the Prime Minister, the Chief of the Defence Force, and the Chiefs of the Army, Navy, and the Air Force. The President of Indonesia presented the Medal of Valour – his country's highest honour – to each of the deceased, placing a medal on each casket.

Survived by her grieving husband and 21-year-old son, Lynne Rowbottom was 43 years old.

David Sutton

Flight Lieutenant Lynne Rowbottom with Naval Reservist Commander Bruce Greig in Dili during their deployment with the United Nations Peacekeeping Force in East Timor, June 2003. Department of Defence

Flight Lieutenant John William Yarra DFM,
No. 453 Squadron, Royal Australian Air Force

Killed in action: 10 December 1942

Flight Lieutenant John 'Jack' Yarra (left) with his brother, Sergeant Robert 'Bob' Yarra, who was also a member of No. 453 Squadron, Royal Australian Air Force, with Jack's Spitfire in England in 1942.

P00943.007

John William Yarra was born in Stanthorpe, Queensland, and attended Grafton High School in New South Wales before working as an apprentice printer for the town's *Daily Examiner*. Known as 'Jack' or 'Slim', he was 19 when he enlisted in the Royal Australian Air Force (RAAF) in October 1940.

After initial training in Australia in April 1941, Yarra was sent to Canada, where he qualified as a pilot. Promoted to sergeant, he was sent to Britain and joined No. 232 Squadron of the Royal Air Force (RAF) in October, and then No. 64 Squadron, RAF, the following month. Flying Supermarine Spitfires, Yarra's first operational flights were fighter sweeps over German-occupied northern France. In January 1942 he was promoted to flight sergeant and posted to No. 249 Squadron, RAF, destined for Malta.

Malta was a vital British base in the Mediterranean. Between 1940 and 1943 the small island was subjected to a siege and bombing from Italian and German aircraft. In March 1942 Yarra was among the first Spitfire pilots who flew off the aircraft carrier HMS *Eagle* to reinforce the island's hard-pressed defenders. A few weeks later he was posted to No. 185 Squadron, RAF, flying Hawker Hurricanes and Spitfires.

The air war over Malta was relentless; Yarra was often in the thick of the fighting, and claimed his first victory on the night of 1 May. It was the first of a series of triumphs: in just over three months Yarra destroyed 12 German and Italian aircraft and damaged six others. In early June he was commissioned as pilot officer, and a few days later he was awarded the Distinguished Flying Medal.

In mid-July 1942 Yarra was posted back to Britain, and joined the RAAF's No. 453 Squadron in September. He had 'a fine reputation' and was one of the most experienced pilots in the squadron, which also included his younger brother Sergeant Robert Yarra. Their time together was brief. On 10 December Jack Yarra was shot down and crashed into the sea off the coast of Holland while attacking a small convoy of German merchant vessels and a flak ship. His body was never recovered. He was 21 years old.

In mid-1942, Jack Yarra wrote a letter to his mother, to be sent in the event of his death. It read:

I entered this war with the knowledge that I had a rather small chance of coming out of it alive. I was under no false impression – I knew I had to kill – and perhaps be killed. Since I commenced flying I have spent probably the happiest time of my life ... Above all, Mother dear, I have proved to my satisfaction that I was, at least, a man.

Dr Karl James

Wing Commander Louis Thomas Spence DFC & Bar, No. 77 Squadron, Royal Australian Air Force

Killed in action: 9 September 1950

Louis Thomas Spence was born in Bundaberg, Queensland, on 4 April 1917. From an early age he excelled at sports, particularly tennis, and he represented his school in cricket and Rugby League.

Spence enlisted in the Royal Australian Air Force (RAAF) in March 1940 and was accepted for flying training. Near the end of his course he was promoted to flying officer and after gaining his wings joined No. 3 Squadron, RAAF, in North Africa, flying Kittyhawk fighters. He was awarded the Distinguished Flying Cross in 1942 for his skills in air combat. Later that year he returned to Australia as an instructor and finished the war in command of No. 452 Squadron, flying Spitfire fighters.

After the war Spence briefly returned to civilian life, but returned to the RAAF in 1946. He was initially posted to Canberra and then to the RAAF College at Point Cook, Victoria, where he was commanding officer of the cadet squadron.

Promoted to wing commander in February 1950, Spence was sent to Iwakuni, Japan, to take command of No. 77 Squadron, RAAF. Initially, his role was to ready the squadron for return to Australia, but when North Korea crossed the 38th Parallel on 25 June Spence readied his squadron for action. It was not long in coming. The North Koreans had great early success, driving South Korean and American forces back to what became known as the Pusan Perimeter.

Spence led his squadron from the front, flying many operations as well as maintaining the administrative duties and other functions of a unit commanding officer. In August 1950 he was awarded the American Legion of Merit by the commander of the US Far East Air Force, Lieutenant General George E. Stratemeyer, and in early September found out that he had been selected to attend Staff College in Britain in early 1951.

On 9 September he led a flight of four Mustangs over Korea in ground-attack missions against North Korean targets still trying to break the Pusan Perimeter. During a low-level ground attack on storage facilities at An'gang-ni, South Korea, Spence's Mustang was seen attempting to pull out of a dive before hitting the ground at high speed and exploding. It was only after allied troops broke out from the Pusan Perimeter a little over a week later that Spence's body was recovered from the wreck.

Wing Commander Louis Thomas Spence was laid to rest in the United Nations Memorial Cemetery at Pusan, South Korea. He was posthumously awarded a bar to his Distinguished Flying Cross, as well as the American Air Medal.

Lieutenant General Stratemeyer remembered Spence as 'one of the noblest and finest officers of any service' he had ever known.

Michael Kelly

Chapter five

Ceremonies for special occasions

Anzac Day is Australia's national day of remembrance, a time to pay tribute to all who have served the nation during war and on peacekeeping operations over more than a century. Remembrance Day offers another opportunity for reflection, when one minute of silence is observed in honour of servicemen and servicewomen who died or were wounded in the line of duty. In addition to recognising individual Australians, the Memorial's daily Last Post Ceremonies allow for commemoration of significant anniversaries, particular groups, and specific wars or operations.

Special Last Post Ceremonies maintain the focus on an individual Australian who served and died, while at the same time connecting to a broader theme. The person chosen for commemoration may have had ties to a nation or cultural group that is not widely recognised in this context, or they may have fought in a less commonly known war event or campaign. They may have served during a battle whose anniversary is being remembered, or represent a unit that suffered great losses. In these cases, Director Dr Brendan Nelson or a representative will often deliver a commemorative address outlining key historical facts to provide background of the event for visitors.

Special Last Post Ceremonies are generally well attended by official guests, veterans, the public, and Australian Defence Force (ADF) personnel. At ceremonies honouring particular battles or units, a large contingent from the ADF is often involved. At an event to honour Explosive Detection Dogs and their handlers, for example, members of the relevant units from the Australian Army's School of Military Engineering and the Royal Australian Air Force flanked the Pool of Reflection along with their canine partners.

PREVIOUS PAGES Explosive Detection Dogs and their handlers at a ceremony honouring Sapper Darren Smith and his dog Herbie, 23 February 2014. PAIU2014/021.27 BELOW Greg Wilson created *Always beside you* after attending the Last Post Ceremony of Sapper Darren Smith and his Explosive Detection Dog Herbie. RIGHT Explosive Detection Dogs and their handlers relax after the ceremony. PAIU2014/021.30

'I realised during Darren Smith's ceremony that he cared more about Australia and his friends than he did for his own happiness or safety. His story touched my heart and soul in such a meaningful way I decided I had to do a painting in memory of him and the family he dearly loved but left behind. I firmly believe the best way to value and appreciate all those who have died defending our freedoms in the past is to make the most of our own lives today.'
Artist Greg Wilson

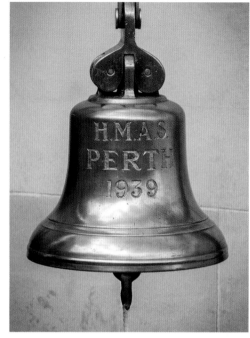

LEFT The medal group of a veteran who served in Malaya and the Vietnam War, worn at the Last Post Ceremony commemorating Vietnam Veterans Day, 18 August 2017. 2017.4.205.59

ABOVE LEFT Sailors from the Royal Australian Navy at the commemoration of the 75th anniversary of the battle of the Sunda Strait, 28 February 2017. 2017.4.27.24

ABOVE RIGHT The bell from HMAS *Perth*. 2017.4.27.4

For the 75th anniversary of the battle of the Sunda Strait on 28 February 2017, sailors from the Royal Australian Navy rang out the bell salvaged from the wreck of HMAS *Perth*. Frequently, Australia's Federation Guard (AFG) conducts a catafalque party for special ceremonies, and ADF chiefs will lay wreaths of remembrance.

Australia's political leaders are present on many occasions, including the special Last Post Ceremony held on the eve of the first day of the parliamentary sitting year. The Prime Minister and Leader of the Opposition, along with dozens of colleagues, stand together to honour a serviceperson who may have also represented the nation as a legislator, or have a personal connection to a current member of parliament.

International leaders, including heads of state, military chiefs, and foreign diplomats, are often invited to attend ceremonies when visiting the nation's capital. The Italian ambassador (along with diplomatic, defence, and veteran communities) was present in November 2015 at the Last Post Ceremony recognising the sacrifice of Italian-born Anzac Private Ferdinando Mottarelli, who served on Gallipoli during the First World War. The commemoration of the 100th anniversary of the Anzac evacuation from Gallipoli, which highlighted the story of Staff Sergeant Harry Bowser of the 2nd Light Horse Brigade, likewise drew a raft of senior diplomatic representatives from countries involved in the campaign: Turkey, Britain, New Zealand, Germany, France, Pakistan, India, and Canada.

LEFT Members of the Italian–Australian Veterans' Association at the Last Post Ceremony to remember Private Ferdinando Mottarelli, November 2015. PAIU2015/189.02 RIGHT Prime Minister Malcolm Turnbull and Opposition Leader Bill Shorten at a Parliamentary Last Post Ceremony in 2016. 2016.8.2.8

War veterans and Victoria Cross recipients frequently attend special ceremonies, and the latter occasionally act as readers. On Remembrance Day 2013, Corporal Ben Roberts-Smith VC MG read the eulogy of the Unknown Australian Soldier, who represents all those listed on the Roll of Honour. This recitation has become customary, and is now delivered each year on 11 November.

LEFT Dignitaries representing several nations lay wreaths at the ceremony commemorating the 100th anniversary of the evacuation of Gallipoli, 20 December 2015. PAIU2015/226.23

RIGHT Keith Payne VC, who received his honour for bravery in Vietnam, has attended several Last Post Ceremonies. PAIU2014/117.17

FOLLOWING PAGES Hundreds of Vietnam veterans attend the ceremony for the 50th anniversary of the battle of Long Tan in August 2016. 2016.8.128.9

'The haunting sounds of 'Danny boy' at the Last Post Ceremony is one of those moments which will stay with me for the rest of my life.'
Rear Admiral Ken Doolan (Retd), former Chairman of the Australian War Memorial

Musical performances also feature on particular occasions. Aircraftman Brodie McIntyre played a didgeridoo at a Last Post Ceremony acknowledging Indigenous Australian servicemen and servicewomen; and pipers of the Canberra Burns Club Pipe Band played 'Highland cathedral' to mark the Memorial's 75th anniversary. One particularly musical ceremony commemorated the 50th anniversary of the battle of Long Tan in August 2016. Musician John Schumann led a performance of 'I was only 19', a song that has become an anthem for the Vietnam War, and Corporal Daniel Keighran VC read the story of Private Kenneth Gant, who died at Long Tan on 18 August 1966. At the end of the reading, a recording was played of Gant singing the Irish ballad 'Danny boy'. He made the record for his mother just before he left for Vietnam as a conscripted national serviceman.

LEFT Aircraftman Brodie McIntyre plays a didgeridoo at a Last Post Ceremony in honour of Aboriginal and Torres Strait Islander servicemen and servicewomen, 7 July 2016. 2016.8.98.7
RIGHT Director Dr Brendan Nelson and his wife, Gillian Adamson, Ben Roberts-Smith VC MG, and musicians Hugh McDonald and John Schumann at the ceremony commemorating the 50th anniversary of the battle of Long Tan in August 2016. 2016.8.147.9

LEFT New Zealand cricket captain Tim Southee and Australian Prime Minister's XI captain Michael Hussey lay wreaths at a Last Post Ceremony on 22 October 2015. PAIU2015/180.13
RIGHT Members of the Australian Olympic Team at a Last Post Ceremony in 2016. 2016.8.145.2
FOLLOWING PAGES Members of the Australian Rules football club the Gold Coast Suns at a ceremony in 2015. PAIU2015.071.18

Last Post Ceremonies can inspire people in different ways. Sportspeople, including Olympians, cricketers, and footballers, have attended these events to draw motivation from the commitment and camaraderie that reveals itself in many Last Post stories. Other attendees have been inspired to undertake further research into military history, to request a Last Post Ceremony for an ancestor of their own, or to produce publications about those who have served and died. Artist Greg Wilson was moved to produce a painting after attending the Last Post Ceremony of Sapper Darren Smith and his Explosive Detection Dog Herbie, who were both killed in Afghanistan on 7 June 2010. Copies of Wilson's painting were subsequently sold to raise money for the charity Soldier On, which supports wounded servicemen and servicewomen.

'*Your officers made us feel as if the story of our relatives was unique, yet we know that they do this every day for every serviceman or servicewoman being commemorated. Their professionalism, enthusiasm, and commitment is exemplary. I would like you to know how much our family members appreciate their efforts.*'
Steve Gavin, descendant of brothers Lance Corporal James Gavin and Private Gavin Gordon Gavin, 26th Battalion, AIF

The ceremonies that involve special guests may assume more formality, but are no less poignant. In 2016 the President of Hungary, János Áder, and his wife, Anita Herczegh, attended a ceremony honouring servicemen killed in Afghanistan. It featured the story of Lance Corporal Luke Gavin, who was killed by a rogue Afghan National Army soldier on 29 October 2011. Gavin's family, including his wife and three children, were present. The First Lady was visibly upset as Gavin's story was read. At the end of the ceremony, Gavin's six-year-old daughter, Olivia, hugged and consoled her.

Special Last Post Ceremonies continue to be held at the Memorial on military anniversaries and for particular groups so that attention may be given to lesser known events or units, thereby providing the public with a greater understanding of the Australian experience of war.

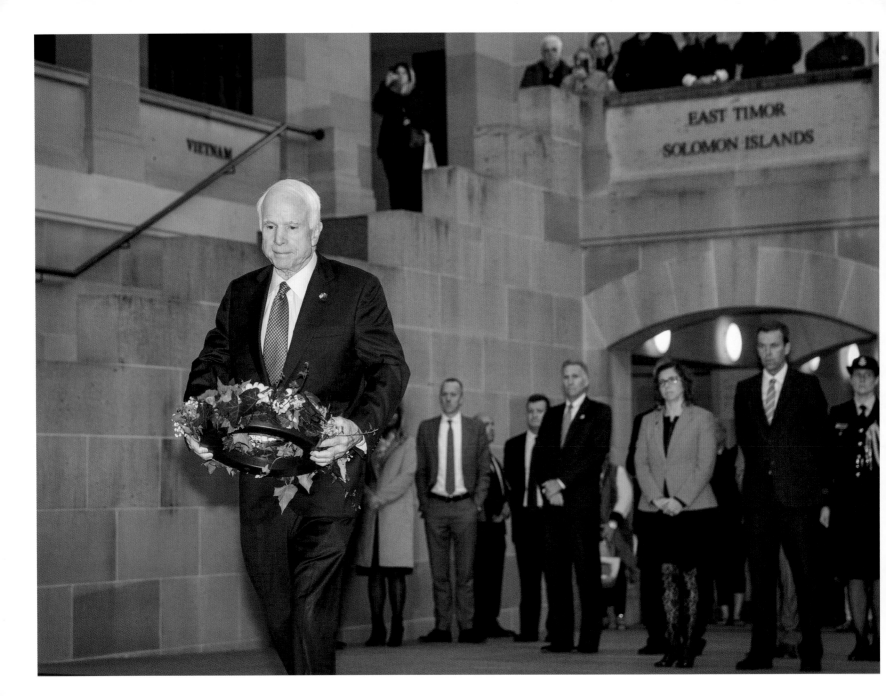

LEFT US Senator John McCain lays a wreath at a Last Post
Ceremony during a visit in 2017. 2017.4.132.32

ABOVE LEFT A wreath laid by France's Veterans' Affairs
Minister Jean-Marc Todeschini, 20 November 2016. 2016.8.211.31

ABOVE RIGHT Indigenous Australian artist Clair Bates at the
ceremony recognising Aboriginal serviceman Lance Corporal
John Hill and the opening of the exhibition *For Country,
for Nation* in 2016. 2016.8.161.1

'The Last Post Ceremony has been the greatest change for the Memorial in the last 40 years. It has enabled the Australian public to feel, once again, connected to our military history through involvement and interaction. It has given relevancy and youth to what is and can be a sombre affair. Current serving military members, veterans, families, and public alike can now interact and be a part of the ceremonies in such a personal way. The Last Post Ceremonies have been able to bring to life individual sacrifices, service, and stories. Being involved in the Last Post Ceremonies at the Memorial I have always been filled with pride, honour, and humility because I know that it is about someone who has gone before us to allow our country to be where it is today.'

Mark Donaldson VC

Sub-Lieutenant Richard Pirrie,
HMS *Copra*, attached to the Royal Navy,
Royal Australian Navy

Killed in action: 6 June 1944

Richard 'Digger' Pirrie's name on the Roll of Honour at the Memorial. 2017.4.278.7

The eldest son of six children born to Richard Francis Pirrie and Isobel Agatha Pirrie, Richard Pirrie was born in the Melbourne suburb of Hawthorn on 6 June 1920. Growing up, he attended St Patrick's College in East Melbourne, and was a promising sportsman, playing three games on the wing for the Hawthorn Football Club before his mobilisation in 1941 with the Royal Australian Naval Volunteer Reserve.

Seconded to the Royal Navy, Pirrie travelled to England, where his British colleagues called him 'Digger'. Based at HMS *Collingwood*, he soon saw action on various destroyers during convoy duties to places such as Russia, Panama, Iceland, and Malta.

Pirrie was promoted to the rank of sub-lieutenant and joined HMS *Quebec*, a flotilla of landing craft. In 1943 he commanded a landing craft in the invasions of Sicily and Italy.

The greatest invasion was to come the following year: D-Day, 6 June 1944, has become an iconic event not only in the history of the Second World War but also in the history of the Western world. On this tumultuous day, a multinational Allied force landed on the shores of Normandy. It was the first major step in the liberation of Western Europe from the tyranny of Nazism and fascism.

The day was also Pirrie's 24th birthday. During the Normandy invasion his landing craft was among the first to approach Juno Beach. Pirrie had been tasked with the dangerous job of piloting his landing craft close to the beach – in full view of the enemy – from where it could direct naval gunfire onto the German defences.

In the hours before the invasion, Pirrie began a letter home to his family. It read:

My dearest Mother, Dad, and the boys. Well, my dears, the pressure is on now and as soon as the weather improves we sail for the greatest event in the history of the world. By the time you receive this you will surely have heard some of the bare details. This is the greatest Armada that ever was formed. A colossal feat of organisation; the product of years of planning and hard work.

The letter was never finished. Pirrie's landing craft was hit by German gunfire, and he was killed instantly.

For his 'gallantry, leadership and determination' on D-Day, Pirrie was posthumously Mentioned in Despatches. His citation stated that he performed his task with great skill, and that 'his conduct and bearing greatly encouraged his men'.

Pirrie was one of thousands of Australians who served in the British and Commonwealth forces on D-Day and throughout the Normandy campaign. He is commemorated on the Plymouth Naval Memorial, which lists the names of 15 993 sailors of the British Commonwealth who were lost at sea.

Dr Lachlan Grant

Staff Nurse Ruby Dickinson, Australian Army Nursing Service, Australian Imperial Force

Died of disease: 23 June 1918

Born in Forbes in New South Wales, Ruby Dickinson was the daughter of William and Julia Dickinson. Following her schooling she trained at the Lister Private Hospital in Sydney between 1906 and 1911.

In June 1914 Dickinson wed Frederick Body, a grazier from Cooma. They had been married little more than a year when she enlisted in the Australian Army Nursing Service (AANS) in July 1915. Only nurses who were unmarried were eligible to join the AANS, so Dickinson used her maiden name.

More than 3000 Australian civilian nurses volunteered for active service during the First World War, most of them with the AANS. They were posted to Britain, France, Belgium, the Mediterranean, India, and the Middle East, where they worked in hospitals, on hospital ships and trains, or in casualty clearing stations closer to the front line.

Dickinson embarked for overseas service within days of enlisting. From September 1915 to January 1916 she was attached to the 3rd Australian General Hospital (AGH) on the island of Lemnos, where her patients included Australians wounded during the fighting on Gallipoli. Conditions on the island were primitive: water was in short supply, there was no sanitation, and dysentery was a scourge. The hospital tents were regularly blown over in the wind and, in cold weather, patients suffered frostbite. In spite of the personal hardships and professional difficulties, the nurses treated and cared for hundreds of men.

After Lemnos, Dickinson spent several months nursing in Egypt. In July 1916 she was assigned as the nurse in charge on the hospital ship *Seang Choon*, which was returning to Australia with sick and wounded men. She left Australia again in January 1917, this time bound for service in England.

In October Dickinson was sent to France, where the 3rd AGH had been re-established. Soon after arriving she became ill and was sent to England to recuperate. She returned to nursing work in January 1918 with the 1st Australian Auxiliary Hospital at Harefield.

Dickinson again dedicated herself to the job, ignoring her own ill health. On 23 June she reported sick to her superiors, and was immediately transferred to a hospital for Australian nurses in Southwell Gardens, London. She died of pneumonia that afternoon.

Dickinson was buried with military honours in the Harefield Parish Churchyard. On 22 October 1918 her mother wrote to the authorities about her daughter:

I am told she was much appreciated for her steadfastness to duty and nursing skills, much beloved by the sick and wounded for whom she worked so hard. I shall always have the consolation of knowing that she died doing her duty.

Ruby Dickinson was 32.

Emma Campbell

Staff Nurse Ruby Dickinson with some of her patients in the grounds of the No. 1 Australian Auxiliary Hospital, England, 1918. H16039

Private Kenneth Howard Gant, 6th Battalion, Royal Australian Regiment, Australian Army

Killed in action: 18 August 1966

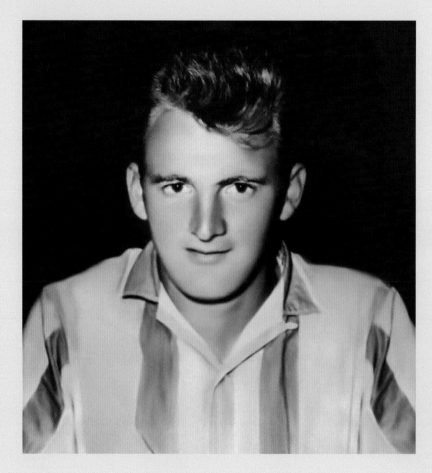

Kenneth 'Kenny' Gant was a
national serviceman in Vietnam.

Department of Veterans' Affairs

Kenneth Howard Gant was born on 6 January 1945 in Brisbane to Harold and Beryl Gant. Known as 'Kenny', he grew up on the family property at Belmont and attended school locally. Later, he went to work as a butcher. Gant was popular in town. He was a good singer, entertaining at local parties, and his friends gave him the nickname 'Bing'.

Gant was called up for service on 30 June 1965. His mother later recalled that he did not like the idea of conscription, but 'he was not a coward' and did his duty.

After a period of training Gant was posted to the 6th Battalion, Royal Australian Regiment, joining 11 Platoon, D Company. While stationed at Tin Can Bay, Gant's company was invited to a dinner by the locals, during which Gant brought the house down with a performance of Roy Orbison's 'Leah'. It was reported that the band had some trouble getting their stage back.

The battalion arrived in Saigon in mid-1966, attached to the main Australian base at Nui Dat. Immediately after arriving the battalion was deployed on a search-and-clearance operation in a nearby village, followed by a five-day search-and-destroy, during which they came into contact with the local Viet Cong D445 Provincial Mobile Battalion. In the early hours of 17 August the base was hit by mortar and rifle-fire, incurring 24 Australian casualties. Patrols were sent out to locate the enemy firing positions, although the Viet Cong had withdrawn.

The following day D Company moved its search into the Long Tan area. Shortly after 3 pm it came into contact with the enemy in a rubber plantation. Gant's platoon began following up the enemy and, at around 4 pm. the Viet Cong opened fire with machine-guns and small arms. During this first attack Gant was shot and killed.

The platoon was now engaged on three sides and was in danger of being wiped out entirely. Monsoonal rain began to deluge the area, reducing visibility and turning the ground into slick red mud. In the hours that followed, the larger Vietnamese force attempted to overrun D Company. Close artillery support was crucial in breaking up several enemy attacks and allowing the beleaguered Australians to bring the scattered sections into a cohesive perimeter. Helicopters flew through the rain to deliver desperately needed supplies.

At 7 pm a relief column of armoured personnel carriers arrived. As they entered the rubber plantation they encountered members of the Viet Cong and attacked quickly, stopping the enemy advance. The carriers linked up with D Company and, as night fell, the enemy withdrew.

Next morning the men of D Company returned to the battle site to recover the wounded. Gant and many of the fallen were found still lying at their weapons, as if frozen in the act of defending their positions.

Gant's remains were returned to Australia, and his funeral was held at the Mount Gravatt Cemetery.

Michael Kelly

Sapper Darren Smith, 2nd Combat Engineer Regiment, Australian Army

Killed in action: 7 June 2010

Darren Smith was born in Adelaide in November 1984, the oldest of three children. He excelled in sport and music, and particularly enjoyed soccer, cricket, and Australian Rules football. He also played guitar in the Wirreanda High School band. To his family, Darren was active and fun-loving, sometimes cheeky, but always well-mannered. A loving son, he was also a devoted big brother to his sisters Chavuanne and Crystal.

Smith always wanted to be a soldier. In 2001 he enlisted in the Army Reserve and underwent basic training at Kapooka, New South Wales. Afterwards he was posted to the 3rd Field Squadron, Royal Australian Engineers, and went on to complete combat engineer training as a specialist in bridge-building, minefield clearance, and demolition. In 2004 he transferred to the Regular Army and was posted to the 1st Combat Engineer Regiment in Darwin. While there, he met Angela. They married and had a son, Mason.

RIGHT Sapper Darren Smith and Herbie in Afghanistan. 2016.153.13
FACING PAGE *Herbie*, by Year 12 student and artist Rachael Michelle Potter, from a series entitled *Unsung heroes – Afghanistan*, 2013. ART96887

Smith transferred to the 2nd Combat Engineer Regiment, and developed a passion for working with Explosive Detection Dogs. Trained to locate improvised explosive devices (IEDs) and weapons caches, these dogs and their handlers form strong bonds.

Smith was paired with Herbie, a two-year-old black-and-tan collie cross. With the possibility of a deployment to Afghanistan approaching, the two trained for six months so they could serve side-by-side.

Smith and Herbie travelled to Afghanistan with Mentoring Task Force 1 in March 2010. Here they conducted foot patrols out of Patrol Base Wali with Mentoring Team Alpha as part of a broader strategy to deny the Taliban access to the Mirabad Valley. Smith and Herbie regularly accompanied the infantry on their daily patrols, sweeping ahead to counter the threat of IEDs.

On the morning of 7 June 2010 the team was conducting a routine foot patrol in and around the village of Sorkh Lez. Herbie, Smith, and Sapper Jacob Moreland were investigating a metal signature in a creek bed when an IED was triggered. The blast killed Herbie, and mortally wounded both Smith and Moreland.

Angela Smith described her husband as 'an absolutely remarkable human being. He was passionate about his job and understood the risks involved, but he was the sort of man who always put others first'. Herbie was cremated in Afghanistan and farewelled by approximately 100 engineers and soldiers of Mentoring Task Force 1. His ashes were transported back to Australia and presented to Smith's family.

Herbie and his handler were commemorated, together with four other Explosive Detection Dogs killed on service in Afghanistan – Merlin, Razz, Andy, and Nova – on a polished metal board in a corner of the Australian recreation area in Tarin Kot, known as 'Poppy's'. Inscribed on the memorial were these words of tribute for the remarkable bond between these loyal dogs and their handlers:

I question not your commands
I follow faithfully wherever you go
I pledge my loyalty no matter what
I share the danger of your terrain
And will readily lay down my life for yours …
for in this moment we are one.

Dr Aaron Pegram

Private Henry Whiting, 3rd Battalion, Australian Imperial Force

Killed in action: 9 August 1918

Private Walter Lewis Whiting, 3rd Battalion, Australian Imperial Force

Died of wounds: 9 August 1918

Henry Whiting was born in 1884 to Richard and Catherine Whiting of Adelong, New South Wales. Known as 'Harry', at the outbreak of the First World War he was farming and taking odd carpentry jobs in the Adelong district. He was a big man for his time, well over six feet and was known to be a very good athlete, cricketer, and tennis player.

Henry's cousin, Walter Whiting, was born in 1893 to James and Annie Whiting, also of Adelong. When war was declared he, like Henry, was farming in the local area.

On 8 August 1915 Henry, Walter, and Walter's brother, Ernest, went to Cootamundra to enlist in the Australian Imperial Force. Walter and Henry were accepted straight away, but Ernest was initially turned down for medical reasons. He tried again the following day and was successful, and the three were posted to the 12th reinforcements to the 3rd Battalion.

Walter, Henry, and Ernest spent longer than expected in camp in Australia because of an outbreak of measles, but finally arrived in Egypt in February 1916. Four months later, after being transferred to France, Walter Whiting came down with meningitis. He became seriously ill and took a year to recover.

In 1917 Ernest Whiting was seriously wounded at Bullecourt. He was eventually declared medically unfit for service and was repatriated to Australia in early 1918.

Walter was also wounded in 1917 near the Belgian town of Ypres. He suffered a bomb wound to his head, and was evacuated to England. For many months he suffered recurring ear and jaw infections as a result of this wound, and was unable to rejoin his battalion until March 1918.

Henry's health also suffered, and he was in and out of hospital over the following years. Nevertheless, he was considered 'one of the finest soldiers who went away' from Adelong, and was spoken about by his mates 'in the highest terms of his qualities as a soldier and a comrade'.

In August 1918, during the great allied advance known as the battle of Amiens, Walter and Henry Whiting were back together in the trenches. Sometime during the early hours of 9 August, a German aircraft flew over their position and dropped a bomb. The blast killed Henry Whiting outright. Walter Whiting suffered a penetrating chest wound in the same blast and was taken to the 7th Australian Field Ambulance Dressing Station. He died shortly afterwards.

Henry and Walter Whiting were buried side by side in the nearby cemetery. Henry was 34 years old; his cousin was 25.

Dr Meleah Hampton

LEFT Private Henry 'Harry' Whiting served in the 3rd Battalion, Australian Imperial Force.
RIGHT Private Walter Whiting of Adelong, New South Wales.

Images courtesy of Sue Beattie

Chapter six

The Australian Defence Force and the Last Post

RIGHT Last Post Ceremonies provide an opportunity to contribute to the remembrance of the dead. PAIU2015/180.25

At each of the Memorial's Last Post Ceremonies, a uniformed member of the Australian Defence Force (ADF) reads the story of the person being remembered, followed by the recitation of the Ode. It is a poignant tribute paid by those who now serve to those who once did.

For decades, the ADF has been involved in commemorative events at the Memorial, including Anzac Day and Remembrance Day ceremonies, battle anniversaries, and plaque dedications. The Last Post Ceremony provides another opportunity for today's servicemen and servicewomen to contribute to the tradition of remembrance. While ADF personnel read the stories, members of the Australian Army Band Corps perform daily in the roles of piper or bugler. Australia's Federation Guard (AFG) conducts a catafalque party and twice a month stations guards at the Tomb of the Unknown Australian Soldier during the event. Participants consider it an honour, a privilege, and among their proudest achievements. 'It's a very profound, touching, sentimental, and humbling experience,' said Flight Lieutenant Guri Singh of the Royal Australian Air Force (RAAF), who has read at more than a dozen Last Post Ceremonies. '[There is] a great sense of pride in having played a small part to acknowledge and honour our fallen.'

'The memory of reciting the Ode, whilst looking gun-barrel-straight down the Pool of Reflection to Parliament House, will remain forever treasured.'
Warrant Officer Shannon Power, Royal Australian Navy

Among those who have read are Victoria Cross recipients and defence force chiefs, but any member – including cadets from the Australian Defence Force Academy in Canberra – can volunteer to take part. Such is the popularity of the Last Post Ceremonies that it is common for ADF personnel to do so multiple times. 'The first time I read I had to hold back tears when reciting the Ode, as it was such a tremendous privilege to be doing it,' said Warrant Officer Class 2 Joanne Davy of the Australian Army. 'If family members are present I endeavour to meet them either before or after the ceremony. It is not unusual to see that they have been greatly affected by the experience.'

ABOVE Warrant Officer John Kinder died in captivity following the horrific Sandakan death march. P06190.001
RIGHT Australian Defence Force Chief General David Hurley AC DSC places a poppy next to the name of Lance Corporal Shannon McAliney after reading his story at a Last Post Ceremony, 30 June 2014. PAIU2014/130.32

It has also become customary for outgoing senior members of the ADF to read at a Last Post Ceremony as one of their final duties. In June 2014, ADF Chief General David Hurley AC DSC delivered the story of Lance Corporal Shannon McAliney of the 1st Battalion, Royal Australian Regiment (1RAR), who died during Operation Solace, a peacekeeping and humanitarian mission in Somalia. Hurley was retiring after more than 40 years of military service, which included commanding 1RAR – and McAliney – during its deployment to the civil-war-torn African nation. Another moving ceremony occurred on Vietnam Veterans Day in 2017, when Major General Stuart Smith AO DSC, Deputy Chief of Joint Operations for the Australian Army, read the story of his father, Sergeant Bernard Lyle Smith, 5RAR, who was killed in Vietnam when Stuart was just five years old. Janice, Bernard's widow, laid a wreath at the ceremony, which also marked Stuart's retirement after more than 30 years of service, and Stuart's brother, Edward, wore their father's medals.

ADF reader Warrant Officer Angelo 'Gus' Augostis had no personal connection to Warrant Officer John Kinder, but was familiar with his story many years before he asked to retell it at a Last Post Ceremony.

Kinder, of No. 1 Squadron, RAAF, was made a prisoner of war when the Australian forces on Singapore Island surrendered to the Japanese on 15 February 1942. After a brief period at the camp in Changi, he volunteered for a working party and was sent to Sandakan, Borneo, to help build a military airstrip. The conditions at Sandakan were horrendous: food was scarce, illness and death ravaged the camp, and the prisoners were often beaten by their captors.

The completed airfield was quickly destroyed by Allied aircraft bombing and so, from January 1945, the fittest prisoners – including Kinder – were forced to march 260 kilometres westward along the mountainous jungle tracks to Ranau. The men were malnourished, and many became ill along the way. The heat was oppressive and the guards refused to let the prisoners rest. Hundreds died from disease or starvation, or at the hands of the guards, who regularly clubbed or shot to death those unable to walk.

Kinder made it to the camp at Ranau, but became weak from dysentery before contracting malaria. The 28-year-old from Ascot Vale in Victoria died on 10 June 1945.

'It is a great honour to be part of the ceremony. It is an opportunity to publicly acknowledge in the most appropriate setting the sacrifice that individuals have made in the service of our country, and it personalises the names on the Roll of Honour.'
Major Matthew Dingley, Australian Army

Of the 2500 Australian and British prisoners of war sent to Sandakan on Borneo's north-east coast in 1942, only six – all Australians – survived. The Sandakan death march remains the single greatest atrocity committed against Australians in war.

Gus Augostis began his career with the RAAF more than 40 years after Kinder died on Borneo. During a posting to Malaysia, he participated in a walk that partially retraced the steps of the Sandakan death march. Augostis was advised that he would be walking in remembrance of Warrant Officer Kinder, so he researched Kinder's story before the trek. In doing so he discovered a man of strong character:

I was impressed by the leadership he demonstrated through his service. Kinder was put in charge of one of the prisoner-of-war parties on the death march and was reported to have received several beatings from the Japanese for protesting about the ill treatment of his men.

Augostis had already read at four Last Post Ceremonies before he requested one for Kinder. He recalled that Kinder's nephew had explained to him that the family had been unable to hold a memorial or funeral at the time of his death. 'They were very grateful that he could be remembered at a Last Post Ceremony ... a fitting way to honour him.'

LEFT A member of Australia's Federation Guard at the entrance to the Hall of Memory. 2016.8.174.4
RIGHT An Australian Defence Force cadet reflects following the ceremony to commemorate the 76th anniversary of the Battle of Britain, 15 September 2016. 2016.8.154.32

ABOVE Royal Australian Navy officers at the ceremony
commemorating the 70th anniversary of the battle of Leyte
Gulf in 2014. PAIU2014/219.44

RIGHT Australian Defence Force members feel privileged
to be able to participate in Last Post Ceremonies. 2017.4.135.2

'Having the honour to be the person representing the fallen is more than anyone could ever ask for. To me these people are the ultimate heroes.'

Trooper J. Carter, 1 Troop,
Australia's Federation Guard

'To walk through the cloisters of the Australian War Memorial and read the thousands of names is to face the sad reality that our freedom has been bought and paid for by those who have made the ultimate sacrifice for us.'
Lieutenant Commander Peter Bartholomeusz, Royal Australian Navy

Lieutenant Commander Annette Nelson of the Royal Australian Navy (RAN) considers the ceremonies an important educational tool, particularly for the many school children who visit the Memorial. 'The readings make the people more real for the students,' she said. 'It is such a solemn, respectful ceremony that may be a totally new experience for some, especially if they do not have a military connection.'

The personal histories of the soldiers, including their 'larrikin pasts', have been a highlight of the Last Post Ceremony experience for Lieutenant Colonel Andrea McMahon, commanding officer of the Australian Army Band:

I love relaying their lives pre-service: just about all of the men I have spoken about were from country Australia and were thoroughly active in their local communities. I'm certain they would have been a significant loss not only to their families but also to the community in general.

Participation in Last Post Ceremonies has led some ADF members to further research individuals from the Roll of Honour, track down relatives of those who have died, and make strong connections with descendants of the fallen. Major Ian Cook researched and wrote a magazine article about the life and service of First World War

soldier Lance Corporal Hector Merton Cornish, whose story he had read at the Memorial. Cornish, a bugler with the 31st Battalion, had died of wounds on 13 March 1917, aged 21. 'I think it is only right that we all learn more about those who went before us and built the foundations upon which we now stand,' said Cook.

Warrant Officer Gerard Gough, RAAF, initiated contact with the descendants of Flight Sergeant William Andrew of No. 9 Squadron, Royal Air Force (RAF), through his in-laws, who lived in Dalby, Queensland, where Andrew was born. The interaction led to Andrew's great-nephew, Neil Andrew, travelling from Dalby to Canberra for his great-uncle's Last Post Ceremony. He later wrote to Gough to thank him for honouring Flight Sergeant Andrew, who had served in the Second World War as a rear gunner on an Avro Lancaster heavy bomber, and was killed when it was shot down by flak off the western coast of France on 13 August 1944. Gough has resolved to read a Last Post story at least once every year – coinciding, if possible, with his own date of enlistment.

In 2014 Leading Aircraftwoman Sarah Love of No. 381 Squadron, RAAF, met a descendant of Second World War air bomber Flight Sergeant Stanley Black while serving as part of the AFG catafalque party at the unveiling of a memorial plaque in Graignes, France. Black, of No. 106 Squadron, RAF, was killed in the Graignes area on 11 June 1944 in the fighting for the village during the Normandy campaign. He was 21 years old. Love kept in touch with Black's great-niece, who asked her to participate as a reader at the Last Post Ceremony held in his honour at the Australian War Memorial a year later. Love recalled:

It was moving for me to see how happy Flight Sergeant Black's family were to be part of the Last Post Ceremony. It means a great deal that these soldiers, sailors, and airmen are acknowledged, as every serviceman and servicewoman makes sacrifices during their career to make Australia the country it is to live in today.

'Thank you for the important work you do, as even after all these years since Bill was lost to the family, we have all wondered what his wartime service entailed, and how he was killed.'
Neil Andrew, great nephew of Flight Sergeant William Andrew, No. 9 Squadron, RAF

LEFT Cadets are often in attendance at special occasion ceremonies. 2017.4.1.1

Commemorating individuals who have died in recent actions can be particularly poignant for serving members. Craftsman Ben Wheadon of 1 Troop, AFG, has participated in around 50 Last Post Ceremonies as a piper and guard of the Tomb of the Unknown Australian Soldier. The ceremony for Lance Corporal Luke Gavin, killed in October 2011, was the most memorable to Wheadon because Gavin 'was a soldier killed in Afghanistan shortly before I deployed there, and it was very moving to see his wife and children lay a wreath in his memory'.

'I feel a close connection with the Australian War Memorial and feel proud that I can play a part in the workings of the institution.'
Warrant Officer Geoff Banning,
Royal Australian Air Force

LEFT Wing Commander (Retd) Sharon Bown at a ceremony honouring peacekeepers in 2017. 2017.4.236.29
RIGHT Interacting with the public after ceremonies is a high point for Australian Defence Force members. 2016.8.154.34

Visitors attending the ceremonies will often approach ADF members to thank them for taking part. For these servicemen and servicewomen, interacting with the public after the event is another highpoint of their involvement in the ceremony. Lance Corporal Courtney Stenchion of 2 Troop, AFG, was part of the catafalque party in an all-female Federation Guard at a ceremony to honour First World War Staff Nurse Ruby Dickinson. The bugler and piper on the day were also women. 'The all-female Last Post Ceremony received many accolades,' Stenchion said later. 'The public reviews were very touching.'

Participation in the Last Post Ceremony by current ADF members is undertaken with a generosity of spirit rather than an expectation of reward. Cadet Harrison Leonard was humbled to read an account of the life and service of Driver Roy Edward Francis Sadler of the 110th Australian Howitzer Battery, who was killed near Messines in Belgium on 14 June 1917 when a German shell hit an ammunition dump and caused a massive explosion. Sadler, from Wee Waa in New South Wales, was just 20 years old when he died. This resonated with Leonard, who enlisted in the RAAF at 19. He said of the experience, 'To me, remembering and appreciating the service of others is an important step in understanding the reality of a life of service, and it acts as a reminder to live according to their legacy.'

'I had the privilege of laying a wreath during the closing of the Memorial in honour of my friend Lance Corporal Andrew Jones (KIA 30 May 2011 – Afghanistan). It was a very emotional experience and one I will never forget. I am so proud that our national heritage is being preserved and honoured by such honourable people.'
Corporal Ben Collison, Australian Army

LEFT Many Australian Defence Force members feel a strong connection to the Memorial. 2017.4.280.1

Private Richard Warne MM, 31st Battalion, Australian Imperial Force

Accidentally killed: 25 August 1919

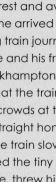

Richard Warne was born in 1898 to Richard and Clara Warne, who owned a property on the edge of the small village of Owanyilla, just south of Maryborough in Queensland. He was educated at the local school and worked on the family farm until March 1916, when he enlisted in the Australian Imperial Force.

Initially attached to the 41st Battalion, Private Warne embarked for England in May 1916. Following months of training, in September he was transferred to the 31st Battalion and sent to the Western Front in France.

In February 1917 Warne was supplying rations to the front line when a shell burst shattered a nearby urn, drenching his feet in boiling water. He was sent to England for specialist treatment, and spent eight weeks at Norfolk War Hospital. After his release he remained in England to help train troops before returning to France in September. A few months later he was sentenced to one day's detention for taking four pounds (1.8 kilograms) of apples to give to his mates.

On the night of 28 July 1918, during an attack on enemy trenches at Morlancourt, Warne volunteered for duty as a stretcher-bearer. Under heavy machine-gun and shell-fire, he carried wounded men to safety, working without food or rest through the night and into the following day, until all of the wounded had been brought in. For his actions he received a Military Medal.

A few months later Warne was part of a three-man Lewis gun team that engaged a German battery holding up the battalion.

For his help in putting the German guns out of action, Warne was recommended for a Bar to his Military Medal. While this was not awarded, he was Mentioned in Despatches.

When the war ended on 11 November 1918 Warne and his unit returned to England to enjoy a well-earned rest and await transport home. Embarking in July 1919, Warne arrived in Melbourne the following month. After a long train journey to Brisbane, on the evening of 24 August Warne and his friend Private George Black set off on another train to Rockhampton.

As they neared home, Warne learned that the train would not stop at Owanyilla. Unwilling to face the crowds at the busier Maryborough station, and preferring to go straight home, he planned to jump off at the platform when the train slowed. In the early hours before dawn, as the train reached the tiny village station, Warne woke Black and said goodbye, threw his kit bag off the train and jumped after it into the dark, his overcoat slung over his right arm.

At about 7 am, a station guard picked up a kit bag a few feet from the platform. He took it to the woman responsible for keeping the railway gates. Curious, she followed along the tracks towards Maryborough, and saw more luggage. A little further on was the body of a man, lying in a rock cutting by the track. The woman sent her sister to the nearest neighbour for help; this turned out to be Richard Warne senior, who lived less than a mile from the station.

Mr Warne followed the woman to the railway track and found his son bloodied and broken, unconscious but still breathing. There was blood on his face, and his right leg was almost severed above the knee.

Richard's mother and younger sister soon arrived at the scene, but Warne never regained consciousness. An ambulance arrived after an hour, and Warne's father was with him as he died on the way to hospital. He was 21 years old.

The local community was shocked by the death; Private Warne had survived the Western Front only to be killed within sight of home. His funeral was well attended, and the people of the district raised funds to erect a memorial over his grave at Maryborough Cemetery.

Emma Campbell

LEFT Private Richard Warne was awarded a Military Medal for his actions as a stretcher-bearer in France during the First World War.
Courtesy of Daryl Kelly

RIGHT The funeral procession for Private Richard Warne proceeds through the streets of Maryborough, Queensland, 26 August 1919.
Courtesy of Daryl Kelly

Captain Robert Charles Page DSO, Z Special Unit, Second Australian Imperial Force

Executed: 7 July 1945

Lieutenant Robert Page, Major Ivan Lyon MBE, Gordon Highlanders, and Lieutenant Donald Davidson, Royal Naval Volunteer Reserve, celebrate in Brisbane in 1943 after the successful completion of Operation Jaywick. 045423

Robert Charles Page was born on 21 July 1920 in Sydney, the eldest son of Harold and Anne Page. Known as 'Bob', he attended Sydney Boys High School and enrolled to study medicine at the University of Sydney in 1940. A little over 12 months later, he left his studies to enlist in the Australian Imperial Force. Joining the 2/4th Pioneer Battalion, he was quickly promoted to lieutenant.

In 1942 Page's father, who was serving as a senior administrator in New Guinea, was captured by the Japanese at Rabaul. Later that year he was en route to Hainan, China, on board the Japanese transport ship *Montevideo Maru* when it was torpedoed and sunk, killing Harold Page and more than a thousand prisoners of war on board.

That same year Robert Page transferred to Z Special Unit, a joint Allied unit formed to conduct clandestine operations behind Japanese lines in south-east Asia. In September 1943 he took part in Operation Jaywick, devised by British officer Major Ivan Lyon and using a dilapidated Japanese-built fishing vessel, the MV *Krait*, to sneak a crew of 14 into enemy waters. The *Krait* left Western Australia on 2 September and arrived off Singapore about three weeks later. From there, Page and five other men paddled canoes into Singapore Harbour and attached limpet mines to Japanese ships under the cover of darkness. The mines destroyed or seriously damaged seven ships and more than 35 000 tonnes of shipping.

Back in Australia, Page married Roma Prowse in Canberra on 1 November 1943. He was awarded the Distinguished Service Order for his 'courage and devotion under extreme hazardous conditions', but because of the need for secrecy, even from his wife, the award was not officially promulgated until 1945.

Meanwhile, a new raid was being planned – Operation Rimau. On 11 September 1944 a party of 23, including the recently promoted Captain Page, were taken by submarine to the South China Sea, where they seized a local junk and made for Singapore. They were discovered, however, and had to abandon the mission. Unable to return to the submarine, the party split up into four groups to try to reach Australia in small boats. Most were killed in intermittent fighting on the way south, and ten, including Captain Page, were captured and taken back to Singapore. Facing charges of espionage, they were tried and found guilty, and were beheaded on 7 July 1945, one month before the end of the war.

Roma later recalled, 'We waited and waited for them to come back, but of course, they never did, and then we waited for something official'. On her second wedding anniversary she received a telegram to say that Robert had died of illness while a prisoner of war of the Japanese. It took many years for her to discover the truth of her husband's role in Z Special Unit.

Robert Page was 25 years old.

Dr Meleah Hampton

Chief Petty Officer Edward Charles Perkins, 1st Royal Australian Naval Bridging Train, Royal Australian Navy

Killed in action: 6 September 1915

Edward Perkins was born on 5 March 1894 in Melbourne to Harry and Emma Perkins. He was one of seven children. Known as 'Ted' to his family and friends, he attended Essendon State School, after which he became an apprentice farrier working for R.J. Laughlin of North Melbourne. He was living with his parents in Essendon when war broke out.

Perkins joined up on 12 April 1915. Prior experience with the Militia engineers and the Essendon Rifles made him a valuable asset to his unit – the 1st Royal Australian Naval Bridging Train. He was immediately made chief petty officer (farrier) and was one of the few men in the unit with horse-handling experience.

The bridging train embarked on 4 June 1915 aboard the transport ship *Port Macquarie*. Originally bound for the United Kingdom, after six weeks the ship was diverted to Gallipoli for the coming offensive.

On Imbros island in late July, Perkins and his comrades trained in pontoon-bridge and pier construction – the main task they would face on the peninsula.

The August Offensive on Gallipoli was the allied attempt to break the existing stalemate and turn the campaign in their favour. While Australian troops launched diversionary attacks, a mainly British force landed further north at Suvla Bay. It was here that Perkins and the Royal Australian Naval Bridging Train were sent.

They landed at Suvla in early August and immediately began constructing pontoon piers on the beach and managing the unloading and distribution of stores, including vital water supplies.

Isolated from the Australians at Anzac Cove, Perkins and his comrades carried out their jobs over the next month with great skill and determination, and were highly regarded by their British and dominion comrades. The bridging train's base at Kangaroo Point was an important supply point and the men were frequently forced to continue their work under enemy aircraft and artillery fire.

During the early morning of 6 September, Kangaroo Point was again heavily shelled by the Turks. During this bombardment, Perkins was killed outright by a direct hit on his dug-out. He was 21 years old.

Perkins's body was buried in Kangaroo Beach Cemetery, but was later reinterred at Hill 10 Cemetery in Suvla Bay.

On the first anniversary of Perkins's death his family published in memoriam notices in the *Argus*. One included the epitaph:

Though the waves of ocean divide us,
And you sleep on a foreign shore,
Remembrance is a relic,
That will last for evermore.

Craig Tibbitts

BRIDGING TRAIN STAFF

Corporal Cameron Stewart Baird VC MG, 2nd Commando Regiment, Australian Army

Killed in action: 22 June 2013

Cameron Baird was born in 1981 to Kaye and Doug Baird in Burnie, Tasmania. He grew up in Melbourne and attended the Gladstone Views Primary School and Secondary College. He was a keen and skilled sportsman, and excelled at discus and shot-put, but his greatest passion was for Australian Rules football. He was captain of the Victorian Schoolboys' Team and won best-and-fairest awards at all junior levels.

A fierce but fair competitor, Baird soon came to the notice of the Geelong Football Club. In his final year of playing for the under 18s, however, he was injured in the shoulder, and was overlooked in the draft for senior players.

Rather than wait a year for the next draft, Baird chose to enlist in the Australian Army. He was turned down twice because of his injury, but succeeded on the third try. He proved a skilled soldier, and successfully passed the physically demanding Special Forces selection process at the age of 19. He was posted to the 4th Battalion, Royal Australian Regiment (Commando) – later known as the 2nd Commando Regiment.

Baird challenged himself constantly, and completed nearly 150 army courses, becoming proficient in handling more than 40 weapons systems. He was never known to ask a soldier to do something he would not do himself. Where possible, he would personally provide support for families of soldiers serving overseas, and was involved in charity work to provide for families and soldiers who were struggling financially.

Baird was deployed to East Timor and Iraq. Disappointed with the lack of action required by Australian troops, he left the army in July 2004, but after a period spent in private security he re-enlisted in September 2006.

Baird made four deployments to Afghanistan. In 2007 he was part of a commando company ordered to search and clear a Taliban stronghold. Lance Corporal Baird's friend and fellow soldier Private Luke Worsley was mortally wounded during an engagement with the enemy. Despite being under heavy machine-gun and rifle fire, Baird took Worsley to safety and went on to reorganise his men and neutralise the enemy guns with grenades, continuing the fight until the stronghold was cleared. For his 'conspicuous gallantry, composure and superior leadership under fire', Baird was awarded the Medal of Gallantry.

On 22 June 2013 Corporal Baird and his team attacked an insurgent network at Ghawchak in the remote Khod Valley of Uruzgan province. Shortly after insertion by helicopter, Baird and his team came under small-arms fire, which Baird was instrumental in subduing. He personally charged an enemy-held building three times. The third time the enemy was destroyed, but Corporal Baird was himself killed while drawing enemy fire away from his team.

He was 32. His acts of valour and self-sacrifice had allowed the Australians to regain the initiative, and preserved the lives of his team members. For this he was posthumously awarded the Victoria Cross for Australia.

A fellow commando later said of Baird, 'For such a big, intimidating dude ... a fearless warrior, he was actually a really gentle man and he did have a big heart'. Warrant Officer Dave Ashley said: 'Corporal Baird's actions epitomised the courage and quick thinking needed to be a commando. He was just a dynamo in that unit ... one of Australia's greatest ever soldiers.'

Baird once told his mother: 'It could happen to me, it could happen to anyone, any time. We know the dangers, but it's our job.' His funeral service was held at the Reedy Creek Baptist Church on the Gold Coast. His parents and brother accepted his Victoria Cross from the Governor-General of Australia in February 2014. The family donated it to the Australian War Memorial, where it is now displayed in the Hall of Valour.

Baird's was the 100th Victoria Cross to be awarded to an Australian.

Dr Meleah Hampton

LEFT Corporal Cameron Baird VC MG.
Department of Defence
RIGHT Corporal Baird's medal group.
OL00649.001

LEFT The Last Post Ceremony for the 100th anniversary of the battle of Beersheba on 31 October 2017 featured a parade of the standard and guidons of the Royal Australian Armoured Corps, which is historically linked to the Australian Light Horse regiments of the First World War. 2017.4.281.55

RIGHT The Memorial by night. 2017.4.154.21

LEFT Minister for Veterans' Affairs Dan Tehan comforts a veteran at the ceremony commemorating the 75th anniversary of the second battle of El Alamein, 23 October 2017. 2017.4.271.43

RIGHT A visitor watches a ceremony from the cloisters. 2017.4.120.3

LEFT Floral tributes by the Pool of Reflection following a Last Post Ceremony in the Commemorative Area of the Australian War Memorial. PAIU2013/155.06
RIGHT Corporal Emma Oleson is helped by a technician prior to reading at a Last Post Ceremony. 2017.4.135.2

Members of the Australian and New Zealand defence forces, along with members of the Brumbies and Highlanders Rugby Union teams, at a Last Post Ceremony in April 2015. Wreaths are being laid by the New Zealand Chief of Army Major General Dave Gawn MBE and the Australian Chief of Army Lieutenant General David Morrison AO. PAIU2015/054.27

List of Last Post stories

Introduction

Private Thomas Anderson Whyte,
10th Battalion, Australian Imperial Force,
25 April 2014

Sister Mary Eleanor McGlade,
113th Australian General Hospital,
Australian Army Nursing Service, Second
Australian Imperial Force, 12 February 2016

Lieutenant Colonel Charles Hercules
Green DSO, 3rd Battalion, Royal Australian
Regiment, Australian Army, 27 July 2013

Lieutenant Anthony Austin Casadio,
Royal Australian Navy Helicopter Flight
Vietnam, Royal Australian Navy,
30 January 2018

Chapter one:
THE ORIGINS OF THE LAST POST

Warrant Officer Class 1 Gordon Wallace
Duff, 2/3rd Battalion, Second Australian
Imperial Force, 24 October 2017

Lieutenant Stanley Spencer Reid,
6th Western Australian Mounted Infantry,
Colonial Military Forces, 28 May 2017

Lieutenant Robert David Burns,
14th Australian Machine Gun Company,
Australian Imperial Force, 19 July 2018

Lance Corporal Shannon McAliney,
1st Battalion, Royal Australian Regiment,
Australian Army, 30 June 2014

Chapter two:
THE AUSTRALIAN WAR MEMORIAL

Chaplain 3rd Class Michael Bergin MC,
Australian Chaplains' Department,
Australian Imperial Force, 17 March 2017

Ordinary Seaman Edward Sheean,
HMAS *Armidale*, Royal Australian Navy,
1 December 2013

Private George Ross Seabrook,
17th Battalion, Australian Imperial Force,
4 April 2017

Private Theo Leslie Seabrook,
17th Battalion, Australian Imperial Force,
4 April 2017

Second Lieutenant William Keith Seabrook,
17th Battalion, Australian Imperial Force,
4 April 2017

Temporary Sergeant Stafford Kenny James
Lenoy, 3rd Battalion, Royal Australian
Regiment, Australian Army, 23 April 2016

Private Tom Jones, 3rd Battalion, Australian
Imperial Force, 3 May 2018

Chapter three:
THE LAST POST CEREMONY

Lance Corporal John Hill, 2/4th Machine
Gun Battalion, Second Australian Imperial
Force, 22 September 2016

Lieutenant Gordon Vincent Oxenham,
No. 1 Squadron, Australian Flying
Corps, Australian Imperial Force,
16 December 2015

Sister Caroline Mary Ennis, 10th Australian General Hospital, Australian Army Nursing Service, Second Australian Imperial Force, 8 May 2018

Private Dal Edward Abbott, 1st Battalion, Royal Australian Regiment, Australian Army, 30 May 2014

Chapter four:
THE FAMILIES OF THE FALLEN

Lieutenant Colonel Edgar Leslie Cecil Willis Walker Maygar VC DSO, 8th Light Horse Regiment, Australian Imperial Force, 1 November 2018

Flight Lieutenant Lynne Elizabeth Rowbottom, Health Services Flight Townsville, Royal Australian Air Force, 2 April 2019

Flight Lieutenant John William Yarra DFM, No. 453 Squadron, Royal Australian Air Force, 4 September 2013

Wing Commander Louis Thomas Spence DFC & Bar, No. 77 Squadron, Royal Australian Air Force, 26 October 2014

Chapter five:
CEREMONIES FOR SPECIAL OCCASIONS

Sub-Lieutenant Richard Pirrie, HMS *Copra*, attached to the Royal Navy, Royal Australian Naval Volunteer Reserve, 6 June 2014

Staff Nurse Ruby Dickinson, Australian Army Nursing Service, Australian Imperial Force, 11 October 2016

Private Kenneth Howard Gant, 6th Battalion, Royal Australian Regiment, Australian Army, 17 August 2016

Sapper Darren Smith, 2nd Combat Engineer Regiment, Australian Army, 23 February 2014

Private Henry Whiting, 3rd Battalion, Australian Imperial Force, 29 April 2014

Private Walter Lewis Whiting, 3rd Battalion, Australian Imperial Force, 29 April 2014

Chapter six:
THE AUSTRALIAN DEFENCE FORCE AND THE LAST POST

Private Richard Warne MM, 31st Battalion, Australian Imperial Force, 1 August 2018

Captain Robert Charles Page DSO, Z Special Unit, Second Australian Imperial Force, 1 November 2013

Chief Petty Officer Edward Charles Perkins, 1st Royal Australian Naval Bridging Train, Royal Australian Navy, 11 December 2017

Corporal Cameron Stewart Baird VC MG, 2nd Commando Regiment, Australian Army, 13 May 2015

Notes

1   Lyndell Bell, 'New Last Post Ceremony for Australian War Memorial', 702 ABC Sydney, 17 April 2013, <www.abc.net.au/local/stories/2013/04/17/3738826.htm>.

2   Alwyn W. Turner, *The Last Post: music, remembrance and the Great War*, Aurum Press, London, 2014, p. 40.

3   *The Age*, 12 November 1919, p. 9.

4   Ian Connerty, *The Last Post: 30,000 daily tributes to the fallen of the Great War*, Uitgeverij Lannoo, Belgium, 2014, p. 16.

5   'Last Post at Menin Gate', Australians on the Western Front, <anzacportal.dva.gov.au/history/conflicts/australians-western-front-19141918/australian-remembrance-trail/ieper-2>.

6   'The daily act of homage', Last Post Association, <www.lastpost.be/en/home>.

7   Alwyn W. Turner, 'The story of the Last Post', *BBC Magazine*, 11 November 2015, <www.bbc.com/news/magazine-34768398>.

8   Turner, 'The story of the Last Post'.

9   Turner, *The Last Post*.

10 Australian War Memorial (AWM) Media Release, 'Memorial launches daily Last Post Ceremony', 17 April 2013.

11 C.E.W. Bean, 'Australian records preserved as sacred things', *The Register*, 7 December 1917, p. 8.

12 Bean, 'Australian records preserved as sacred things'.

13 Anne-Marie Conde, 'The Australian War Records Section', <www.awm.gov.au/blog/2007/06/12/the-australian-war-records-section>.

14 Michael McKernan, *Here is their spirit: a history of the Australian War Memorial, 1917–1990*, University of Queensland Press, Brisbane, 1991, p. 61.

15 Peter Londey, 'Known soldiers: the Roll of Honour at the Australian War Memorial', in Martin Crotty (ed.), *When the soldiers return: November 2007 conference proceedings*, University of Queensland, Brisbane, 2008, pp. 261–69.

16 McKernan, *Here is their spirit*, p. 145.

17 'Honour Roll installation at Memorial', *The Canberra Times*, 21 March 1961.

18 Emma Campbell, 'All of them, one of us: the Unknown Australian Soldier', <www.awm.gov.au/blog/2013/11/04/all-them-one-us-unknown-australian-soldier>.

19 Campbell, 'All of them, one of us'.

20 Kangaroo Valley A&H Association, *One hundred years of achievement, 1885–1985*, p. 18, <kangaroovalleymuseum.com/sites/default/files/pdf/KVAH-Association-Centenary-Transcription-A5-web.pdf>.

21 Richard Reid, 'Sergeant Eric A. Tate, 20th Battalion, AIF', *Wartime 1*, November 1997, p. 16.

22 Eric Tate (Sergeant), private record, AWM: PR90/096.

23 Eric Tate to Emma Tate, AWM: PR90/096.

24 Eric Tate to Emma Tate, 9 May 1916, AWM: PR90/096.

25 Eric Tate to George Tate, AWM: PR90/096.

26 Eric Tate, AWM: PR90/096.

27 Tate, Eric Austin, National Archives of Australia (NAA): B2455.

28 2926 Sergeant Tate, Eric Austin, Australian Red Cross Society (ARCS), wallet 7, Wounded and Missing Enquiry Bureau files, 1914–18 war, 1DRL/0428, RCDIG1031421.

29 Sergeant Herbert Inman to Emma Tate in Eric Tate, AWM: PR90/096.

30 The recitation (including the Ode), <www.awm.gov.au/commemoration/customs/recitation>.

31 Hugh Poate, email to Emma Campbell, 22 August 2017.

32 Chris Wright, email to Dr Brendan Nelson, 28 August 2013.

33 Joan Quinlan, letter to Dr Brendan Nelson, 24 March 2017.

34 Interview with Vin and Nancy Cosgrove, conducted by Emma Campbell on 16 August 2016.

35 Jim Dickson, letter to Dr Brendan Nelson, 6 January 2014.

36 Jim Dickson, letter to Dr Brendan Nelson, 6 January 2014.

37 Robert Keady, letter to Dr Brendan Nelson, 28 February 2016.

38 Phil Taylor, email to Last Post Ceremony team, 1 December 2016.

Acknowledgments

This book would not have been possible without the assistance and support of many people. Firstly, I thank Dr Brendan Nelson for his support of the concept for a book about the Last Post Ceremony, and his encouragement as the manuscript took shape.

I thank Hugh and Janny Poate, Mark Donaldson VC, and Ben Roberts-Smith VC MG for their considered reflections on the ceremonies. Vin and Nancy Cosgrove also generously gave of their time to be interviewed on what the daily event means to families.

I am grateful to the Australian Defence Force for its support, particularly in allowing members to respond to questions regarding their involvement in the ceremonies. Special thanks to Paul Cottier and Geoff Banning for coordinating the responses.

Thanks to Daryl Kelly for providing photos and information about Private Richard Warne, and to Richard Pirrie for his efforts to provide photos of his uncle, Sub-Lieutenant Richard Pirrie. I am likewise appreciative towards the families of Gordon Duff, the Whiting cousins, and Kenneth Gant for granting permission to use images of each of their relatives.

Assistant Director Anne Bennie has been a champion of this book, and Catriona Smith, Chris Widenbar, and Cathryn Rodriguez have kindly provided assistance required in an executive capacity.

I also recognise my many colleagues at the Memorial who have contributed to this work. In particular, I thank the talented team in the Military History Section, who write the biographies, as well as the dedicated Last Post Ceremony administrative team of Erica Bozsoky, Jodi Hammond, and Jennifer Surtees, who provided intricate details about the day-to-day running of the event. The Memorial's Commemoration and Visitor Services team, led by Sarah Hitchcock, gave thoughtful insights into the ceremonies and their impact on the public.

The extraordinary images in this book are the result of the creative and production talents of the Memorial's multimedia and photography team: Kerry Alchin, Steve Burton, Adam Kropinski-Myers, Bob McKendry, Ian Roach, Fiona Silsby, Daniel Spellman, and Andrew Taylor. Special thanks to Steve and Bob for their patience and help with this momentous collaboration.

Mark Campbell and Ron Schroer were instrumental to this project through the administration of publication arrangements.

I gratefully acknowledge the support and encouragement of Ashley Ekins, Head of the Memorial's Military History Section, and the camaraderie and good humour of my colleagues: Duncan Beard, Michael Bell, Lachlan Grant, Meleah Hampton, Karl James, Michael Kelly, Andrew McDonald, Annabel McWhinnie, Aaron Pegram,

Thomas Rogers, David Sutton, Craig Tibbitts, Haruki Yoshida, and Christina Zissis. Former colleagues Kate Ariotti and Steven Bullard also supported the book by contributing biographies, and Peter Burness provided much encouragement. Special thanks go to Meleah for championing me as author, and to Lachlan for reading and commenting on the manuscript.

Particular praise must be given to Christina for her tireless editing work throughout, her astute suggestions to improve the narrative, and her attention to detail. It is a far better book because of her.

At NewSouth I am grateful to Elspeth Menzies, and Deborah Nixon, who saw this book through to production. I am particularly grateful to Justine Molony for her diligence in editing the manuscript, her comments, and her feedback.

Finally, I thank my family: my parents and siblings, for their support and encouragement; my sons Finn and Sam, for their love and enthusiasm; and my husband Pat, who read and commented on numerous drafts, and also gave me the time and space to work on this project. Words cannot express how lucky I am to have you in my corner.

Tribute quotes featured throughout this book have been drawn from thank you letters and emails received by the Australian War Memorial, and interviews conducted by the author.

Index

LEFT The mosaic interior of the dome of the Hall of Memory by artist Napier Waller. PAIU2015/052.02

PARKER J. L.	THOMAS A. E.	MARTIN H.	SHEPHEARD R. W.	WEITEMEYER H. W.
PARRY J. H.	THOMPSON A. H.	MARVEN C. W.	SHERRY P. R.	WHALAN A. E.
PATTERSON W. R.	THOMPSON S. W.	MATHESON R. L.	SIGUT E. L.	WHITCOMBE W. J.
PEACOCK H. G.	THOMSON R. K.	MAURER A.	SIM J.	WILDER C. F.
PEARCE G. W.	THWAITES G. W.	MAWHINNEY G. W.	SIMPSON C. R.	
PENNO L. W.	TIPPETT G.	MICHAEL J. J.	SIMPSON F.	
PETERS S. T.	TIVEY E. P.	MIDGLEY H. W.	SINGLETON D. B.	2/26 BA
PHELPS G. M.	TODD A. R.	MILLAR W. P. G.	SINGLETON K. D.	
PLUNKETT R. L.	TRAIT J. A.	MILLMAN D. A.	SINNOTT A. J.	ADAMS A. H.
POLLOCK W. H.	TRAVERS F. McQ.	MINCHIN M.	SLATER G.	ATKINS F. L.
PRETTEJOHN C. G.	TREWIN R. C.	MOFFAT E. G.	SLAVIN W.	ATKINSON E. S.
PROWSE H. A.	TRICKETT C. P. W.	MOLONEY J. M.	SLUGGETT R. W.	BAGLEY E. F.
QUINN K.	TRIPLETT L. C.	MONGER E. J.	SMART C.	BAKER W. T.
RANSOME J.	TURNER D.	MOORE W. C.	SMELCHER T. R.	BANCROFT E. D.
RATHJEN E. S.	TYSON W.	MORRIS A. B.	SMITH A. J.	BANNAH V. J.
RAYMER A. N.	URQUHART G. F.	MULLINS F. J.	SMITH C. G.	BARBER G. K.
REDFERN S. M.	WALKER D. J.	MURPHY P. V.	SMITH E. S.	BARKER D. T.
REES G. C.	WALL R. E.	NASH J. W.	SMITH G. H.	BARKLE C. H.
REID R. K.	WALLIS E. V.	NEILSON A. B.	SMITH N. R.	BARWICK W. J. B.
RIDGEWAY H. J.	WATERS C. H.	NIGHTINGALE J.	SMITH P.	BATES H. J.
RIXON T. E.	WATSON E. P.	NIXON T. B.	SMITH S. E.	BAUMAN G. H.
ROBINSON E. L.	WATSON S. J.	NOONAN R. J. C.	SMITH T. G.	BAZZO J. V.
ROFFEY D. F.	WAUGH L. A.	NUTT A.	SMYTH D. J. G.	BEATON F. M.
ROSELT E. C.	WEBB H. G.	O'NEILL T. S.	SPENCE G. E.	BEHAN K. H.
ROUSSAC L. A.	WERNDLY C. C.	OPPY H. D.	SPENCE W. A.	BEITZ G. V.
ROWLAND C. A.	WHITAKER G. T.	O'RAFFERTY P. J.	SPITTALL L. C.	BELLAMY G. J.
RUDOLPH A.	WILKINS H. T.	ORMSBY D.	SQUIRES R. H. C.	BENHAM E. J.
RUSSELL T. J.	WILLIAMSON E. A.	PAGE W. J. T.	STRATTON S.	BENNETT A. E.
RUTHERFORD J.	WILLIS D. J.	PARK D. R.	SULLIVAN W. J.	BENSON A. H.
SELLARS W.	WILSHIER K. L.	PARKER J. A. W.	SUPPLE J. C.	BERESFORD J. E. A.
SHIELS B. T.	WILSON E. F.	PARKINSON J.	TARR K. H.	BERG F. J.
SIMPSON F. W.	WILSON P. G. T.	PARRY J. A.	TAYLOR A. P.	BICE C. J. S.
SMEDLEY D.	WINDEBANK G. A.	PATERSON F.	TAYLOR R. H.	BIDSTRUP N. M.
SMITH C. L.	WINDLEY R. E.	PATERSON W.	TEESE H. L.	BIGNELL S. K.
SMITH F. J.	WINWOOD R. W.	PAULL D. K. M.	THALBOURNE M. D.	BILLSBOROUGH H. W.
SMITH M. R.	WOODS G. E.	PAYNE M. K.	THOMAS G. F.	BLACKWELL J. LE T.
SMITH W. H.	WOODWARD K.	PAYNE S. P.	THOMAS V. C.	BLACOW W.
SPINK A.	WRIGHT G. W.	PEARSON H.	THOMPSON L. L.	BLAKE R. A.
STEPHENSON W. J.	YOUNG G.	PELHAM D.	THORNBURY K. D.	BLANNIN S.
STEWART R.		PELLING A. C. J.	TIDESWELL H.	BOESE R. J.
		PENNEY L. E.	TRAVIS G. B.	BOLT R.
		PHILLIPS H. O.	TRIPP L. J.	BOON J. C.
2/24 BATTALION		PHIN J. W.	TRYHORN A. W.	BOURKE W. J.
		PLASTOW E. A.	TURPIN E. G.	BOWERS J. E.
ABBOTT D. W.	FRANKLIN G.	PLUNKETT M. O.	TYE W. F. W.	BOWKETT E. J.
ADAMS S. L.	FREAME H. W.	POLLARD W. J.	UREN P. M.	BOWLING T. J.
AHERN F. W.	GAZZARD L. H.	POWER C. J.	VAINS G. M.	BOYES A. H.
ALLEYNE F. O.	GERAGHTY E.	PRYDE R.	VIVIAN H. N.	BRADFORD R.
ANTHONY C. G.	GIBSON I. H.	PURSE H. C.	WAGHORN C. E.	BREEN P.
ARGALL E. A.	GILDAY J. G.	QUIGLEY J. F.	WAKEHAM V.	BRENNAN J. T.
				BROCKHURST A. W.